THE LITTLE BOOK OF
ROOTWORK

THE LITTLE BOOK OF ROOTWORK

A BEGINNER'S GUIDE TO HOODOO

Including Candle Magick, Rituals, Crystals, Herbs, and More

PARIS AJANA

"The Hoodoo Goddess"

ULYSSES PRESS

Published by:
ULYSSES PRESS
PO Box 3440
Berkeley, CA 94703
www.ulyssespress.com

ISBN: 978-1-64604-187-9
Library of Congress Control Number: 2021931510

Printed in the United States by Versa Press
10 9 8 7 6 5 4 3 2 1

Acquisitions editor: Casie Vogel
Managing editor: Claire Chun
Project editor: Tyanni Niles
Editor: Renee Rutledge
Proofreader: Barbara Schultz
Front cover design: Chelsea Hunter
Interior design: what!design @ whatweb.com
Artwork: © Ardea-studio/shutterstock.com
Layout: Jake Flaherty
Contributing writer: Acacia Harris

NOTE TO READERS: This book has been written and published strictly for informational and educational purposes only. It is not intended to serve as medical advice or to be any form of medical treatment. You should always consult your physician before altering or changing any aspect of your medical treatment and/or undertaking a diet regimen, including the guidelines as described in this book. Do not stop or change any prescription medications without the guidance and advice of your physician. Any use of the information in this book is made on the reader's good judgment after consulting with his or her physician and is the reader's sole responsibility. This book is not intended to diagnose or treat any medical condition and is not a substitute for a physician.

This book is independently authored and published and no sponsorship or endorsement of this book by, and no affiliation with, any trademarked brands or other products mentioned within is claimed or suggested. All trademarks that appear in ingredient lists and elsewhere in this book belong to their respective owners and are used here for informational purposes only. The author and publisher encourage readers to patronize the quality brands mentioned in this book.

Every day, I give my thanks to my ancestors, especially my beloved Grandma Mary Ree and my dad for passing down the traditions to me.

Thank you to my loves Dorden, Soleil, Nova, Sage, and my dearest mom.
I appreciate your love and support every single day.

I love y'all forever.

CONTENTS

PART ONE

GETTING STARTED

OPENING LETTER TO READER

Dear Beautiful Soul,

I am beyond grateful that I have the opportunity to meet with you energetically as you dig deeper into your inner calling. Curiosity is perhaps your soul and spirit communicating, nudging you to rise to the occasion while embracing the process of your awakening. Whether your beloved ancestors directed your movements by whispering in your ears or are sending signals to your third eye, you are here for a reason.

Thank you for being here; I welcome you to your magickal and spiritual journey. We are all spiritual beings with an innate intelligence to receive abundance in all forms in the time and space of our human experience. We can create, build, and live the life we desire and deserve as God has intended for all of us. The key is to learn how to receive and take action through the proper channels, regardless of how smooth or bumpy your path. Enjoy the adventure of enlightenment.

You may have heard stories of your ancestors who practiced hoodoo or felt immediately drawn to a variety of magickal practices. You are here to learn. Embrace that yearning to align your inner truth, magick, and your spiritual beliefs together. It may take time to harness your abilities and learn which materials, techniques, and tools work best for you. It takes patience, diligence, and courage to face your challenges and strengths. Even if you come across an unfavorable outcome, there will be something more fulfilling that is already on its way to you. Sometimes, lessons and repeated lessons are there to clear the obstacles and resolve any karmic debt. Keep in mind always to celebrate the little victories that you achieve and manifest toward you. These little manifestations are just as great as the magnificent ones. If you are open to receive, then it was all in divine timing for you.

As you begin, allow yourself to be open to receive new information for **Part 1: Getting Started**. You'll learn more about the history of rootwork, basic terminology, and my own experience on my journey. Then, you'll learn about must-have materials and tools for your magickal and spiritual journey ahead.

You will then move to **Part 2: Beginning Rootwork**. This section will focus on creating an altar and sacred spaces in your home and office, and as you travel. Next, you'll dive deeper into herb magick and how you can incorporate different herbs to make floorwashes, spiritual baths, incense, powders, and oils. Crystals and stones were not as common in traditional rootwork practices. Only a select few were used for protective amulets and added to mojo bags to increase their powers. Today, crystals and stones are incorporated more frequently in daily self-care routines, rituals, and spells. This specific topic is covered in detail in this book for you to work and build a partnership with the spirit of nature's gift to us in the form of a crystal or stone.

Part 3: Intermediate Rootworking will teach you more about amulets, charms, and talismans. You'll start to notice that you may have these types of items already. Sometimes, you are not aware of the magick that you unconsciously practice. Think about the imbued heirlooms that you receive with your beloved ancestor's energy and spirit. You care for them and keep them safe. You are aware of how special and unique those items are to you because of that energetic connection. Think of this connection as you learn how the blend of Native American traditions and Christianity with hoodoo came to be. Even if you are not religious, you will grow to understand how the Bible and the power of prayers assisted our ancestors on multiple levels. With this information, you'll learn how saints and other spirits can help you with your rituals, spells, and spiritual journey.

As you combine parts 1, 2, and 3, you'll be ready to learn how to write petitions and which materials to use. Then you'll know which colors influence chemical, emotional, and physical changes to our environment, and even to us. Each color is imbued with powerful energy and is also associated with astrological signs. This information will give you the ability to customize your rituals and spells intrinsically for you and other people.

Part 4: Advanced Magick is the final section, taking you a step into the future of your craft. Even if you feel that you're not quite ready to move to this part, it's essential to read. You'll know what to look forward to once you're prepared to proceed to this level. With the knowledge from parts 1, 2, and 3, you will craft the perfect rituals and spells that work for you. You can look forward to working with the energy of the moon, plus which days of the week will work best for your goals and intentions. After that, you'll learn other rituals and spells on how to prepare candles, honey jars, mojo bags, and spirit dolls. Then you'll know how divination can be a part of your magickal and spiritual practice. Using bones, candles, cards, or even pendulums as divination tools, you'll see which ones you gravitate toward building a lasting partnership with along your journey.

Through this book, I believe I can help you understand where to begin and how to advance toward your goals. You'll build a solid foundation by recognizing your energy and power. You'll hear your ancestors speak more loudly to you daily, even if at first you're not aware of their voices and signals. You'll see that any fears you may have with moving forward don't compare to the number of ancestors that you have supporting you. You'll feel their power surrounding you once you start to become aware of their energies. Each material, technique, and tool that you partner up with is energetically there to serve you at that time. You'll build confidence by using my rituals then start to create your rituals and spells. You'll go from unconsciously unaware to consciously aware once you complete this book and practice your craft. You'll be ready to step into this new awareness as a rootworker.

Blessings,

Hoodoo Goddess
Paris Ajana

CHAPTER 1

ROOTWORK: THE POWER OF FOLK MAGICK

MY MAGICKAL AND SPIRITUAL JOURNEY

Every day, I begin my morning with God and my ancestors. I do my best to live a God-centered life because they are my keys to strength and success. I can't imagine not listening to my ancestors' guidance and continuous prodding to expand beyond my limits. Life wouldn't feel right if I ignored the signs, symbols, and synchronicities I see daily. They whisper in my ear to stay positive, even when times are disordered.

Over the past decade, being actively present in my spiritual journey, I learned to tune out unwanted energies and noise. In this voyage of self-discovery, I started to see the world through a higher level of consciousness and received access to information that seemed to come out of nowhere. I will forever give my ancestors my thanks and praise for putting me here because I learned to trust the process and believe that everything comes in divine order, as it should be. This is the heart of my rootwork practice.

Rootwork allowed me to improve my life with rituals. Through it, I've been able to identify and heal from generational traumas. I then moved to connecting more deeply to and building a partnership with the energies and spirits of specific materials and tools. Rootwork has become intertwined with my whole life. Particular parts of my life, like the flow of money, the presence of love, and the connection to the spirit world have shifted toward the better. The power of rootwork allows abundance to flow toward me freely in all directions and forms.

WHAT IS ROOTWORK?

Also referred to as "hoodoo" or "conjure work," rootwork is the spiritual work that originated from the ancestors of Africa. During the transatlantic slave trade, Africans were packed on ships bound for America, separated from their homeland and forced to mix their traditions with others.

Hoodoo began to mix with the culture and magick of Native Americans. White Americans sought to convert Africans and African Americans to Christianity. Their descendants who followed hoodoo found ways to hide their culture without being persecuted, syncretizing hoodoo with certain aspects of Christianity to conceal their traditions in secrecy. In essence, hoodoo is folk magick, powered by the blood and tears of African ancestors.

PURPOSE OF ROOTWORK

Rootwork calls upon the supernatural essences. It is the practice of connecting with spirits in the celestial sphere. It entwines with the use of natural objects, such as bones, herbs, stones, and roots, and other things that hold innate power. In the rootwork philosophy, every object—abiotic or biotic—has a spirit host with particular intentions and uses. Throughout the book, I will refer to this spirit as a spirit guide. For example, keys can open doors and locks in the physical realm, so keys can open new opportunities and gates to new pathways in the spiritual realm. The spirit in the keys helps the user unlock a problem.

Rootwork branches out in purpose; it is up to you to respectfully use rootwork and its powers. Rootwork is the harbinger of new opportunities based on how you choose to incarnate them. Rootwork can help you find prosperity, repair or find love, protect against evil spirits, and call upon the guidance of another wisdom. Culturally, rootwork connects the user to the souls in Africa.

HOW DOES IT WORK?

In order to use the benefits rootwork offers fully, you must identify your purpose. Are you gambling and need extra luck? Are you going on a date and hope for a successful experience? Are you hoping to heal a family member from bedevilment? After you pinpoint your purpose, the next step is to find the perfect objects to help you fulfill your needs. Every item has a different embodiment, as you will learn later in the book.

Rootwork only works when you respect the spirit, and it respects you. You must also find peace with yourself to be at peace with your spirit guide. Trust, respect, and offerings are essential to enacting rootwork successfully. It's key to remember that the more you give, the more you get. Popular offerings to the spirit of the objects you conjure include but are not limited to food, money, rum, and tobacco. The more of these offerings you give the object you're working with, the more it will support your purpose. For example, when using herbs and employing their energy, tobacco smoke snaking up their roots would be most effective.

Without the necessities of trust, respect, and offerings, the rootwork practice can go astray, especially if your purpose is not truthful or clear. When calling a spirit, approach it with reverence and love, emotion and sentimentality rather than logic or observation.

ELEMENTS OF ROOTWORK

The elements of rootwork are vast. Emotions, physical and spiritual objects, and spirits meld to create rootwork's achievements. It's best to be utterly transparent while exercising rootwork. Again, if you give offerings and respect to the spirits you call on to help you, you'll find the outcome miraculous.

Physical elements of rootwork include bones, plants, stones, and inanimate objects with particular purposes, like an ax or money. While using these articles, feel your emotions and clear your mind of worries and wonder. Be purposeful in your intentions and confident in your connection with the spirit world to enact rootwork in the best possible way.

HOW IS IT DIFFERENT FROM VOODOO?

Misconceptions between hoodoo and voodoo are common. Hoodoo is the magick that originated in Africa but evolved to include cultural elements from Native Americans and Christianity. Voodoo is a religion that stems from Africa and has ceased to dwindle. It has many names and ideas, as voodoo was not the original spelling. "Vodou" is the cultural spelling of voodoo that masters of the religion use.

CAN ANYONE PRACTICE HOODOO?

Hoodoo is a magickal practice, and these practices are open to anyone willing to exercise them. Although hoodoo stems from African ancestors, anyone can call upon spirits given the right offering. Hoodoo practice uses candles, charms, herbs, mojo bags (also known as gris-gris), oils, and other objects. These objects can be charmed, made, found, or collected by anyone and everyone. There is no limit to this magickal practice that can bring love, luck, prosperity, and protection to the user. It just takes the right mind to manifest the benefits.

COMMON ROOTWORK TERMINOLOGY

Before you begin, it's a good idea to become familiar with the following rootwork-related words and phrases that appear throughout the book:

* **Amulet:** A natural material object similar to a charm that aids magickal properties to protect the wearer against an entity such as evil, harm, or illness.
* **Anoint:** To apply or rub oil on a person, place, or thing that is prepared for ceremonial or magickal practices.

- ✳ **Blessing:** To perform a consecration ritual and technique.

- ✳ **Conjured oil:** A consecrated oil for ceremonies, rituals, and spells.

- ✳ **Conjure water:** Water mixed with herbs, oils, and minerals; used for cleansing the home or workplace to increase chances of luck and success or get rid of negative energies.

- ✳ **Crossing and uncrossing:** Terms referring to adding and removing hexes, blockages, or negative energy. Uncrossing spells, baths, and rituals are to cleanse and purify you of curses, hexes, and jinxes.

- ✳ **Curse:** A spell intended to do harm to an individual.

- ✳ **Divination:** A fortune-telling technique to prophesy the future or gain insight with the use of tools.

- ✳ **Doll baby:** A spirit doll created for ritual or spell work.

- ✳ **Dressing:** Similar to anoint but mostly used when referring to candles.

- ✳ **Feeding:** A technique to give a recharging effect to a specific spell—like the mojo bag.

- ✳ **Floorwash:** A Florida water, holy water, and/or herb-soaked water that you use on floors to cleanse, purify, and protect the space. Floorwashes can also be used to hex or to attract a specific energy, including love, money, or peace.

* **Honey jar:** A spell contained in a bottle with honey and other ingredients to direct a positive outcome and to sweeten up an individual.

* **Mojo bag:** A spell packed with ingredients in a drawstring bag to attract or dispel specific intentions. Also known as charm bags or gris-gris bags.

* **Offering:** A specific item given to spirit(s) as an exchange or to show gratitude for their services. Offering items can be placed on the altar or left at a specific location and can be food and drink, money, a candle, or incense, depending on the spirit and the service done.

* **Oracle:** A type of divination, most often used similarly to tarot cards or with runes (a medium used to receive messages about a situation from the divine).

* **Orisha:** African spirits that originate from Yorubaland and are also associated with Haitian Vodou and Louisiana voodoo spirits.

* **Personal matters:** A general term pertaining to personal clothing, hair or nail matter, or bodily fluids.

* **Petition:** A request written to a spirit in the form of a query, letter, or statement.

* **Smudging:** A ritual using the smoke from wood, herbs, or resin to purify or neutralize any energy in a space. Most commonly used are sage, palo santo, copal resin, and lavender.

* **Spirit guides:** A spirit that aids in your protection and guides you through your path of life. Spirits can be ancestors, a guardian angel, and/or your higher self.

* **Talisman:** An object made during specific planet and star cycles that aids powerful properties to bring good luck toward the wearer.

* **Tarot:** A form of divination that uses cards to give clarity on a situation.

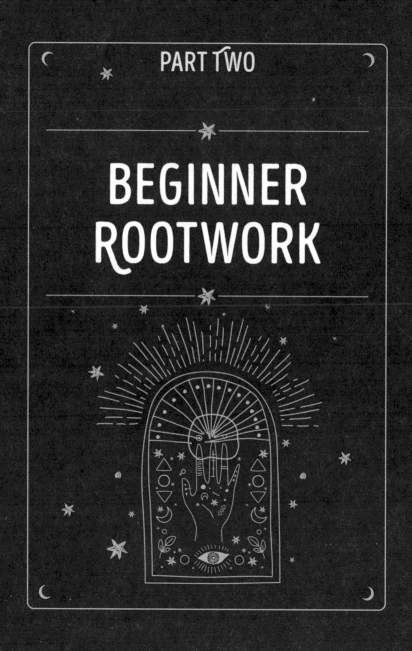

PART TWO

BEGINNER ROOTWORK

CHAPTER 2

✳

ALTARS AND SACRED SPACES

✳

The word altar comes from the Latin word altus, meaning high. Altars are structures with spiritual significance, used in many religions and spiritual practices to connect with personal motives or high spirits; hence, the original meaning. Altars can vary in size, material, design, and divinity.

As you may have seen in sacred places such as a church or a temple, altars are dedicated to remember and honor a religious or spiritual figure such as a high deity, spiritual teacher, or saint. Other altars used in the home or office may include the ancestor altar, love altar, money altar, and an altar used for personal matters. There is no limit to how many or what type of altar you may have.

Your main altar, or your general-purpose altar, is the altar that you frequent the most and can be used for whatever you need at the time. You do not have to separate your altar and create others. If you have specific intentions and wish to create other altars, such as a money altar for finance purposes or a love altar for matters of the heart, or you're limited on space and wish to create a small altar, then I highly recommend that. There are no standard requirements as to what an altar should look like if you are practicing hoodoo. However, you may need some essential items to build your altars for your rituals and spells. These are the basic items you need for any altar: altar cloth, candles, flowers, holy water, incense, picture or statue of a religious or spiritual figure, smudging tools, and table. You should pick items that will assist you with your interconnection with the spirit world.

The very first step to prepare an altar is to go within your own heart. Give thanks and praise to your loved ones, ancestors, and spiritual guides. No matter where you are or what you're going through, you can always go within to commune with God. An altar will help you establish this connection.

CHOOSING A LOCATION

To begin, choose a location for your altars. Find a quiet, peaceful place in your home, office, backyard, or other personal space, where you will not be disturbed. This area needs to be private. If you must disconnect from electronics, please do so to avoid any noise disturbances during your time in prayer, especially if you're performing rituals and spells. Once you have completed your main altar, you may decide to create other altars throughout your home as you see fit. If you practice a particular religion or spirituality, there are specific areas in your home to place these altars. See page 165 for some altar locations in your home for specific orishas.

If possible, have your altar or sacred space positioned so that you face the sun as it rises in the east. According to ancient principles, the sun is a source of life, power, and the divine. The east also has Christian roots as being the direction of Eden.

If you ever find the need to reset the energy flow in your home, look at the blueprint of your home and compare it to a Feng Shui Bagua Map. The setup of the map enhances the flow in the house if you follow it accordingly as a guide. My African American and Filipino family members use the map to place and position furniture a certain way inside the home to create balance and harmony. This map is suitable for maintaining an open flow of energy throughout each room as the flow expands toward the entire house. Your altars will benefit from this map because once you have everything else set up, the flow will be continuous and align with your desired lifestyle.

PURIFYING ALTARS AND SACRED SPACES

Start by cleaning your altar space and wiping down the area before setting up. Always do your best to keep the altar space clear of clutter and maintain it weekly, if not daily. Permanently remove any dead flowers and plants. Keep living plants happy and healthy to keep life and vitality around your altar. Just as you'd give someone fresh flowers and attempt to maintain a garden, you should show respect to your altar and spirit(s) the same way.

ANCESTRAL ALTARS

Honor your ancestors by creating an altar or sacred space for your ancestral line. It is vital to keep your ancestral altar separate from any other altar. You also want to make sure that there are no living individuals in photos placed on this altar, since this is specifically for ancestors who are already in the spirit world, although this may vary by tradition in hoodoo. From the beginning, clarify that you only want well-intentioned ancestors welcomed in your space to serve your highest good. You are allowed to let your ancestors know who is not accepted.

As you begin this journey, learn more about your ancestor's favorite items, drinks, food, hobbies, and music. This information will help you handpick the perfect objects for the altar. Remember, you can start with simple objects and eventually add on as time goes by. You will begin to experience a life-changing journey while connecting and developing a stronger bond with your beloved love ones.

CREATING ANCESTRAL ALTARS

Here are the basic materials and supplies you'll need:

* Anointing oil (see Chapter 8)
* Candles (see Chapter 14)
* Crystals or stones (see Chapter 9)
* Fresh flowers or plants
* Holy water (see Holy Water and Floorwash Formula on page 63)
* Incense burner
* Offering containers (Tupperware containers, old jewelry boxes, ceramic containers, etc.)
* Parchment paper
* Photos of ancestors
* Ritual pen (specifically used or made to write petitions, for candles, or for other magickal purposes only)
* Sacred instrument (bell, drum, harp, rattle, etc.)
* Smudging tools (sage, palo santo, spiritual waters or sprays)
* Statues or pictures of religious figures

* Symbols (amulet, charm, talisman); (see Chapter 10)
* Table
* Tablecloth
* Water bowl or chalice

DAILY ALTAR

Create an altar for daily use and for performing your rituals and spells. Always keep your altar clean and prepared. Maintain a good number of candles for all purposes. In addition to candles, use the same basic materials and supplies as needed from the ancestral altar materials list above. Also, you may want to keep a prayer specific to your intentions at your daily altar.

ALTARS FOR LIMITED SPACES

Does space limit you due to your living situation? Do not worry because there is always a solution. The altar space can be on a bookshelf, countertop, dresser, shelf, or small side table. If this is not available, you may create an altar inside a box, a sturdy gift box, a jewelry box, or even a small chest. I do not suggest that you burn any candles in a box or any small space that may be a potential fire hazard. Considering the room, you may also have to scale down on your altar space objects. Instead of having regular size candles, use tealight candles as a replacement. You may replace incense sticks for palo santo sticks or a sage bundle. Use an abalone shell for storing your smudging tools. Instead of having a statue, view a printed photo instead. Also, consider smaller plants such as bamboo plants for tighter spaces. Use shot glasses for water and offerings. There are many ways to scale down to accommodate an altar in your living space, regardless of square footage.

Examples of limited spaces are:

* Dorms
* Rented rooms
* RVs
* Shared rooms
* Tiny homes
* Vans

OUTDOOR ALTARS

An outdoor altar may be limited in terms of what you can add to it, but there are always solutions for a beautiful setup. Consider the landscape of your front or backyard for placement. If you are limited to a patio or balcony, use outdoor furniture and outdoor accessories to set up your altar. Also, make sure that the space used for your altar is quiet. Using a canopy is a great solution to prevent any sun damage to your altar. If you desire to keep photos outside, make extra copies and get the photos laminated. Think about using outdoor candles and never leave them burning unattended. Leave offerings out with caution unless you want visiting critters. Lastly, consider using specific plants that have a relaxing aroma and a natural bug repellent, like lavender or peppermint, to surround your space and help keep little critters at bay.

Here are some outdoor altar placement possibilities:

* Deck
* Garden area
* Greenhouse
* Patio
* Shed
* Treehouse

TRAVELING ALTARS

If you are always on the road or travel for work, create an altar within a beautiful jewelry case or container to travel with you on the go. You can scale down on the objects and allow enough room to keep all of the essentials together. When I was a child, I used a beautiful 12 x 7-inch jewelry case that was gifted to me by my grandma to keep all my magickal tools together. To this day, I still have my traveling altar with me.

These are some items that make good traveling altar cases:

* Basket
* Jewelry box
* Keepsake box
* Small container (e.g., shoebox)

MONEY ALTARS

Create a money altar for daily use and for performing all matters related to money rituals and spells. Arrange some basic materials and supplies from the ancestral altar list and choose which items fit your intentions best. Is your goal to generate more income? Obtain a promotion or new employment? Or are you allowing yourself to be open to receiving abundance in all forms? Take time to reflect on what you truly desire and arrange your altar accordingly. Remember always to keep your altar clean and prepared. Maintain a good number of money candles, incense, and herbs for money-drawing purposes.

Here are the additional items to place on a money altar:

* Good luck charms
  * Lucky rabbits' foot
  * White elephant

* Good luck plants
  * Four-leaf clovers
  * Lucky bamboo
  * Money tree

* Good luck statues
  * Buddha
  * Elephants with upward trunk

* Good luck symbols
  * Horseshoes
  * Keys
  * Shooting stars

* Money
  * Checks
  * Coins

* Precious Metals
  * Gold
  * Platinum
  * Silver

LOVE ALTARS

Create a love altar for daily use and for performing love rituals and spells. Arrange some basic materials and supplies from the ancestral altar list, choosing which items fit your intentions best. Is your goal to strengthen your current relationship? Obtain a new love? Or even attract more loving relationships in your life that will be fulfilling and serve your highest good? Take time to reflect on what you truly desire and arrange your altar accordingly. Remember to always keep your altar clean and prepared. Maintain a good number of love candles, incense, and herbs for love purposes.

Here are additional materials to place on a love altar:

* Crystals and Stones
  * Rose quartz
  * Malachite
* Love charms
  * Jewelry
  * Magnets
* Love symbols
  * Ankh
  * Heart
  * Love knots
* Romantic plants
  * Carnations
  * Orchids
  * Roses

HEALING ALTARS

Create a healing altar for daily use and for performing all healing rituals and spells. Arrange some basic materials and supplies from the ancestral altar list, choosing which items fit your intentions best. Is your goal to realign your energies for balance and better health? To obtain spiritual guidance from your guides to assist with energetic healings for clients, family, and friends? Or even to break generational trauma with the power of prayers and rituals? Take time to reflect on what you truly desire and arrange your altar accordingly. Remember to keep your altar clean and prepared. Maintain a good number of healing candles such as white candles and chakra candles, incense, and herbs for healing purposes.

Here are additional items to add to a healing altar:

* Chakra tools
* Crystals and stones
  * Amber
  * Amethyst
  * Black tourmaline
  * Quartz
* Essential oil diffuser
* Feathers
* Himalayan salt lamp
* Meditation tools
  * Quartz crystals
  * Singing bowls
  * Tibetan bells
* Oracle cards
* Plants
  * Chamomile
  * Lavender
  * Peppermint

CHAPTER 3

HERBS AND ROOTS

Plants have assisted the human race for generations. They are one of the primary sources around the world, used for nutrition, medicine, and livelihood. Without plants, many medicines and treatments would have yet to exist. When our African ancestors arrived in the United States, they discovered the magick of the land and the plants. They developed trusted relationships with Native Americans, learning additional knowledge and traditions from them. The future of rootwork flourished from the gift of understanding the powers of the native plants.

In rootwork, we honor plants and work with their energy and individual spirit to assist us with rituals and spells, from drawing in new love and attracting more to dispelling unwanted energies from our homes. Each plant has a specific power, and you can depend on using plants to increase strength and connect to a higher level of intent.

In exchange for their magick, we honor plants by giving offerings, prayers, and respect. These offerings may vary; you may provide healing food such as a fresh and natural fertilizer, grounded coffee, or crushed, washed eggshells to help the plant grow in abundance. You may need to research a plant species for guidance on proper care. Keep your plants healthy, and you can ensure they will continue to provide their magick. Another offering is coins. They can either be placed on the soil or in front of the plant. Lastly, liquor, such as rum, and tobacco smoke are common traditional offerings in rootwork. Traditionally, liquor and rum are "sprayed" onto the plant. You take a sip and spray/spit it out at the altar/amulet/talisman. You can also pour it into a cup or spray it with a spray bottle. For tobacco smoke, you can blow the smoke from your mouth onto the plants/objects. Even if you cannot buy the traditional offerings due to age or lifestyle choices, the power of prayer will suffice. Take time to connect with the energies of the plants, and you will learn what you will need to provide in exchange. It's all about reciprocation.

Plants are energy, and they require us to respect what they have to offer. We need to continue to honor their medicine just as our ancestors did. Some cannot see the energy pulsing from nature with the naked eye, but you still should respect it, even when you physically cannot see its energy. As you build a relationship with plants, you'll begin to sense their subtle energies. Once you decide on the ingredients you need, ask the plants for permission to use their gifts. Place your hand on the plant and gently roam around it to see which petals, leaves, branches, or roots will release. If you do not feel connected with the plant, give thanks and move on to a different one. Place your hands around the herbs or roots you choose to acknowledge and thank them for their partnership.

In the upcoming chapters, you will learn how to use specific herbs and roots for many rootwork rituals and spells, including candle magick, honey jars, mojo bags, and spirit dolls. Plants and water are the main ingredients in floorwashes and spiritual baths. Incense, oils, and powders also include herbs and roots as primary ingredients. You'll learn how to dress candles with proper herbs and roots to fulfill your intentions.

WHERE TO FIND HERBS AND ROOTS

In rootwork, the herbs and roots used in rituals and spells can be fresh or dried. It may surprise you that the most common herbs found in your kitchen, such as basil, bay leaves, cinnamon, and cayenne pepper, have multiple functions.

Look for specific herbs at a botanica, health food store, local farm or nursery, or new age store. Depending on where you live, you may find them locally in the wild if you choose to forage for fresh herbs. Since you will be handling plants with your bare hands, ideally, it would be best to choose organic plants in their purest form, free from any harmful chemicals like pesticides. Organic farm products may be more pricey than nonorganic herbs and roots, but I highly suggest investing in higher-quality ingredients for the planet and for your well-being.

If you have the space and ability, the best way to get herbs and roots is to grow them directly. This way, you'll have total control of the growing and harvesting process and will truly benefit from their multiple uses.

When combining your herbs with oils, which we will discuss in further detail in Chapter 8, I recommend using dried or powdered herbs over fresh herbs to prevent oils from going rancid or growing mold. It's always better to use powdered herbs or dried herbs in any formula that will be stored. If you make a lot of a recipe or intend to use it more than once from the same batch, dried or powdered herbs are preferable. Fresh herbs are better for very small batches or a one-time-use batch.

You can also explore the properties of plants and materials imported to the United States, benefiting from the medicine of different regions.

Here is a list of imported plants you can obtain:

* Angelica root (from Europe)
* Benzoin, frankincense, and myrrh (from Somalia and the Middle East)
* Cinquefoil
* Copal resin (from Central and South America)
* Egyptian blue lotus
* Imphepho (from South Africa)
* Galbanum
* Job's tears
* Spikenard

HERBS AND ROOTS AND THEIR ASSOCIATIONS

There are many different herbs and roots out there. Below is a quick guide of the several kinds that exist and how they can be used in rituals, spells, and charms.

Adam and Eve root is a fantastic root that comes in two parts. It is a common root for love rituals and spells. The Adam root is longer and gives the impression of a phallus for the masculine energy. The Eve root is round, providing the power of the divine woman's genitalia. Each of the lovers would carry one part of the root to keep the flame of their love true and to cast down any antagonist working against them. Should someone carry both, they will begin to magnetize desirability, attracting a love and marriage proposal. *USE: Add Adam and Eve root to a love honey jar recipe and a mojo bag for love.*

Alfalfa is a plant that is primarily used to feed livestock and as medicine because of its high mineral content. Alfalfa is used in money workings. It draws prosperity, abundance, and protection from any famines. *USE: Burn alfalfa, use it as an amulet, or put it on your altar to avoid losing income.*

Allspice is also known as the Jamaica pepper, which can come in powder form or whole. It can be utilized in all different forms of rituals based on one's intentions. Allspice allures luck, draws healing to the user, and gives the user the power to obtain desired treasures. You can use this alone when invoking your intentions; however, it can also be included with spells and charms to magnify them. *USE: Add allspice powder to a spiritual bath formula for healing and prosperity.*

Anise star pod is an eight-pointed star that has many uses. Many believe it can spark clairvoyance. It can also be used for those who seek happiness, purification, and aid in health concerns. It is not limited to protection against the wickedness of evil. *USE: Add anise star pods to a handwashing formula for purification.*

Basil is immeasurably more than an herb for the chef in the kitchen; but it's also an arsenal for many magickal purposes.

For business and matters of finance, it can aid in attracting money, success, and prosperity. You may also apply basil in order to attain peace, harmony, happiness, and love. Basil can also drive away bad spirits by protecting those who use it. *USE: Add basil leaves to a blend of money herbs as a dressing for a love or money candle.*

Bay leaf, referred to as "the wishing leaf," is smooth to touch and wide enough to make it the perfect natural surface to inscribe a petition directly onto the leaf. Those seeking assistance with their divination powers have been known to use the bay leaf for this specific reason. Work with basil to keep away danger, harm, and evil. In addition, use it to boost healing, recovery, strength, and success. *USE: Write your success goals on a bay leaf and place it inside a mojo bag for success, strength, and healing.*

Bergamot is believed to increase balance and stability. Many people who have their heads in the clouds call on this supportive herb. Bergamot encourages a tranquil night of sleep and removes interference as well as increases protections from evil and illness. Bergamot is extremely powerful in regard to success and prosperity. *USE: Add bergamot leaves or essential oil to an oil blend for success, balance, and prosperity.*

Catnip is associated with cats or deities. Devoted to Bast, a popular Egyptian goddess, it can be utilized for finding good luck, attracting benevolent spirits, and even luring in love when the herb is infused with roses. Catnip is believed to have the power to enhance beauty and happiness for those who deeply desire them. While in slumber, folks may seek protection from the support of the catnip as well. *USE: Add catnip herbs to rose petals to create your own love sachets.*

Cayenne pepper's vibrant red color alludes to power energy with an instant pungent aroma. For those who seek the assistance of chasing away negativity, ensure that cayenne pepper is on hand and ready to do its work. Folks who find themselves in the midst of a divorce and/or separation will find this to be of great assistance. Cayenne can also be used to cleanse and purify. Should you merge this with other mixtures, it will expedite the process. *USE: Add cayenne pepper when dressing candles for cleansing and purifying.*

Chamomile is more than just the crowd favorite for tea sippers; it's also a gentle herb that will benefit those who are exploring love. When used in a love spell, chamomile has the ability to deepen the connection between an existing relationship. It can be used to draw or bond people by emotional connection. Chamomile doesn't necessarily attract love as it does prosperity. Prosperity is not limited to material wealth, as one can also be prosperous in love and friendship. It draws good fortune in regard to financial matters and those who wager in the game of chance. Chamomile can also be used to support relaxation as a stress reliever and can help digestive health issues. *USE: Boil some spring water in a teapot. Once done, add a tablespoon of organic chamomile flowers* *and recite your desires and goals. As you steep the herbs for 3 to 7 minutes, visualize your intentions coming to fruition. Pour a cup of chamomile tea and sip away.*

Chili pepper is often used in love charms and spells. Many have called on its protective properties to guard them and ward off unwanted individuals. This ingredient is known to be a powerful tool in countering magick, with the ability to break hexes against you. Chili pepper is used to add heat to spells. This amplifies the intensity and pace of the spell. If used in hexing spells, chili pepper can make people physically sick and extremely anxious. *USE: Add chili peppers to candle dressings or jar spells to counter spells against you.*

Cinnamon is used for those looking to support and evolve their spirituality. It calls for the awakening of innate psychic abilities. Cinnamon can also heal and strengthen its users. Like many other herbs and roots, it can protect and provide positive vibrations. Some may also choose to utilize cinnamon for drawing wealth, success, and good fortune. *USE: Add cinnamon sticks to your purse or bag for protection against malevolent spirits and/or to attract wealth.*

Clove is highly fragrant and deeply magickal. It is powerful in protection, having the ability to expel dark spirits and eradicate any negative forces working against an individual. Clove can tame the tongues of those who spread malicious gossip and halt hearsay. On the upside, clove can be of service with love, mental clarity, luck, and financial abundance. *USE: Add clove to a red candle to halt slander and dishonesty to your name.*

Comfrey is said to be the keeper of protection for those who travel. It is known to bring good fortune along with stability and endurance energies. It has a substantial amount of healing properties. Many generations have used it for this exact purpose—to heal on multiple levels. Comfrey is also believed to bring success in divination and the pursuit of goals. *USE: Add dried comfrey to your vehicle by storing it under the seat or hanging it for protection.*

Coriander is utilized to prevent headaches, illnesses, and diseases. Many people work with coriander to help protect against health afflictions. It can also be used to draw in new love, stimulate devotion to ensure fidelity in marriage, bring about, reconciliate, and ease pain from broken relationships. *USE: Add coriander seeds to your attire or carry it in a satchel to prevent disease. It is also a great love herb to add to honey jars.*

Dill is a very protective herb that is used to protect against being cursed and to stop nightmares. *USE: Add dill to floor-washes or protection herb powders to keep negative entities and energy at bay and calm the mind, which is useful for sleep. Or mix dill with damiana, valerian root, lavender, and mugwort for an effective sleep tea or sleep pillow.*

Fennel seeds are used for sexual vitality and long-lasting health. They are known to be used as an herb to increase sexual libido and the overall vitality and youthfulness. *USE: Place in a sachet or mojo bag and carry it around to ward off bad health or increase sexual energy.*

Fenugreek is a powerful and aromatic ingredient that can bring wealth and prosperity to those who use it for money magick. It magnetizes the flow of money toward one's home. Fenugreek is used to root oneself with powerful, protective energies. This heavily supports the amplification of people's intent and their attraction toward you. *USE: Add fenugreek seeds to your floorwash formula or honey jar to draw prosperity and abundance into your home or business.*

Five finger grass is most traditionally used for matters of gambling and luck. Carrying five finger grass and High John the Conqueror root is said to make the hand you hold it in lucky. *USE: Five-finger grass can be added to candle dressings to increase your luck and ensure money will flow your way.*

Frankincense is well known, used by many religious and spiritual figures, including the kings who gifted it to the son of God in Christianity. Frankincense is said to be powerful enough to work with exorcisms and cleansing and purification purposes. It has been used to enhance magick energies in regard to the ego and self-control, as well as help with effective communication skills and concentration when in deep reflection. Creating a sacred space with the frankincense is common. *USE: Add frankincense to satchels for blessing and protection spells.*

Galangal root is used for protective work as in removing curses and evil spells. It supports individuals who seek help with legal disputes and promotes the opportunity to become highly favored in court rulings. This powerful ingredient should improve clairvoyance and be of assistance with health matters. Galangal root is also said to be great for multiplying money for those who desire financial gain. *USE: Add a bundle of galangal roots with money on a money altar for it to multiply.*

Garlic is powerful and is used for many purification purposes. It amplifies protection by driving out negative spirits and energy and ill will. It's a great arsenal for exorcism as it is a healer and can be consumed to expel disease. Folks believe this simple ingredient can strengthen family connection as well as heighten willpower. *USE: Add garlic powder to protection and cleansing spells.*

Ginger promotes optimal health and has powerful protective properties to repel evil spirits. This herb also plays a role in love affairs, spicing up sexuality and passion. Ginger's properties have been utilized to draw in new adventures. Many individuals call on its power as a personal uplifter to either gain self-confidence or reach success and overall prosperity. *USE: Add ginger to love oils and powder to fuel emotions of desire.*

High John the Conqueror is one of the most well-known roots in the hoodoo tradition. According to one traditional story behind the root, High John was a prince from Congo who was sold to North America during the slave trade. He constantly outsmarted the people around him and would play tricks on those who did him wrong. He is known in folklore as a trickster hero who people call on for luck and help to get out of bad situations. *USE: Soak this herb in an oil and apply it to candles, use it as an addition to other spells, or keep it in your pocket to attract luck, protection, and success.*

Horseradish is a powerful root used for its protective abilities to ward off and banish evil entities. *USE: Carry it on you as a protective talisman to keep negative energies or spirits from you, or add it to your floorwash to bring peace to your home.*

Hyssop is said to be the very best herb to utilize in the cleansing and purification process. While that is debatable, its magickal properties are undoubtedly mighty. Some consider hyssop to be the "holy herb," which cleanses holy, sacred spaces. It's also believed to induce the release of spiritual opening for those who seek spiritual growth. Hyssop is also on hand for those who wish to rid themselves of any jinx and to end crossed conditions that an enemy has cast. *USE: Add hyssop to a spiritual bath for its cleansing and healing abilities.*

Juniper berries are traditionally used to ward off thieves and liars, and to attract love. *USE: For love purposes, you can turn the berries into a necklace or bracelet, crush the berries and add the powder to candle dressings, or soak the berries in oil. You can take leaves or bark from a juniper tree and place it above or near valuable items to protect them from being stolen.*

Lavender has a distinctive floral aroma that is used in many love spells. In promoting healing, peace, and tranquility, lavender has been known to help repair individuals who are ball and chained by depression. Happiness and harmony are among its workings. In addition, this herb promotes luck, money, passion, and protection. *USE: Add lavender buds to herb bundles along with incense for cleansing purposes.*

Lemon balm is used to raise and elevate spirits. Known to many as a mender of broken hearts, it has the ability to improve mental and nervous disorders. Some work with the herb to achieve success or aid in love matters. For instance, they may use it to attract a romantic partner if they deeply desire one. *USE: Add lemon balm to boiling water to create tea, which relieves stress and tames anxiety for restful slumber. Also, add lemon balm to love honey jars.*

Linden is the essence of deep affection and love, which is why it plays a very active role in love spells. It emphasizes energies on compassion, protection, and purification. Linden has the ability to distribute healing energies that can see through any healing ritual. It is believed to aid in peaceful slumber for those who are plagued by insomnia. *USE: Add fresh or dried linden to any desired table to maintain good health and to keep one's spirit thriving.*

Mandrake is a great ingredient to add to a honey jar ritual kit since it has the ability to attract. Many people have stated it is absolutely powerful in regard to protection matters, such as guarding homes. Some folks have called on the mandrake in exorcism to remove evil. With its resemblance to the human form, it is no surprise folks create love dolls with the mandrake to lure and attract love as well. This root can also bring prosperity and fertility, preserve health, and, not to mention, reveal God's honest truth. *USE: Add mandrake root as an aphrodisiac herb to enhance desire, fertility, and love rituals.*

Mugwort is known to have a similar scent to sage. With mighty powers and a profound connection to femininity, this herb is known to encourage fertility and strong desire. It's also believed to assist with opening the mind's eye to visions and dreams. Many seek the assistance of mugwort for the ability of astral travel. Mugwort can increase power to help with mental illness. It serves as protection from dark entities from spirit realms. *USE: Hang mugwort on your doorway to repel negative energies from entering.*

Mustard seeds are commonly known in the Bible as references to courage and faith. Mustard seeds are best used to instill inner courage and inner faith during times of hardship and distress. *USE: Place the seeds in a sachet or talisman, and wear it as a good luck charm.*

Myrrh can bring peace. Many people use it as one of their go-to ingredients for cleansing and purifying sacred spaces. It has also been used to bless magickal instruments, awaken spirituality, and increase psychic vibrations. It can be used in meditations to aid in healing. Myrrh is said to be a source of protection by banishing hexes and curses. *USE: Add myrrh to an incense blend to cleanse sacred spaces.*

Nutmeg, also known as Myristica, assists in justice for legal matters, protection, and the ability to repel those who are not wanted. It promotes clarity of the mind's eye, helping with visions for those who seek to enhance clairvoyance. Nutmeg is also said to be the go-to for those who seek luck in the game of chance. Many believe that it can magnify the attraction to prosperity, including love for those who desire it. *USE: Add nutmeg to a mojo bag to draw money and good luck.*

Orange peel is great for stabilizing the mind for the ability to be decisive. Love energy is no stranger to the orange peel, so do not be surprised to see this ingredient in the hands of hopeless romantics. Those who are conjuring up their desires can depend on it to assist in luck, abundance, and prosperity. Many who desire blessings for their home or business endeavors work with this element to ensure success. The orange peel has been used in many ritual cleansings. In addition, it has the power to elevate you spiritually. *USE:*

Add orange peels with floral herbs for an inspiring self-care ritual bath.

Palo santo amplifies positive energy with powerful healing effects. Many people feel that it is deeply sacred and spiritual, as it is used for cleansing and purifying purposes, hence its being referred to as the "holy wood." This element is an absolute favorite when trying to dig deep during meditation for a stronger bond. Many seeking good fortune can use the aid of the palo santo as well. *USE: Add palo santo to your tools for clearing and cleansing sacred spaces by lighting it for 30 seconds and blowing out.*

Parsley is capable of alluring lust when used in rituals, and it is an absolute fertility enhancer. This herb is not just something to reach for when looking to bear children but can be used in many other ways, such as to promote opportunities by encouraging new ideas. Parsley draws in prosperity and luck and increases finances. It also emanates the power to terminate misfortune and serves as a protector. *USE: Add parsley to a warm bath to get rid of misfortune energies.*

Patchouli is known to have a magnetic force when it comes to love. Set meaningful intentions and use it to draw in money and financial support. It's believed to help with business matters for growth and upward mobility. It can also be utilized as an anchor to ground those who are in need of stability. This earthy herb has been called on for fertility help as well. *USE: Add patchouli herbs as a dressing on a candle for money and love spells.*

Pepper (black) is a crucial ingredient and tool used by many spiritual warriors for protection as well as attack magick. Pepper is said to have the ability to repel negative vibrations, release jealous thoughts and feelings, and aid in turbulent or difficult situations. It is definitely an item worth having around and ready. *USE: Add pepper to a candle for protection or cleansing spells.*

Peppermint has extremely powerful purification and healing properties. It is believed to clear sickness and expel negative energies. Many utilize peppermint to aid in mental clarity, which can enhance your third eye. People seeking assistance with prophetic dreams often lean on peppermint for these reasons. Financial matters and success matters also benefit from peppermint magick. *USE: Add peppermint to incense blends for mental clarity. Also, add peppermint to money spells for financial gain.*

Pine has anchoring abilities to keep one grounded when in need. Some gravitate to pine for the support to stay on course. While radiating strong protective properties that can block negative energies, pine can be a key player in warding off evil. It provides strength for those who require the support, and it promotes fertility. Pine has been the go-to ingredient for those who desire new beginnings, success, growth, and prosperity in health. *USE: Add a pine branch to your altar space to sweep away negative energies.*

Rose is said to bring good luck, which enhances love and promotes romance. It aids in bringing friendships closer, helping to build enduring relationships, bringing peace energies, and increasing happiness. *USE: Add rose petals to a spiritual bath for all matters of love.*

Rosemary has a distinctive and inspiring aroma. Those who seek good health typically utilize rosemary for its healing properties. Many believe that it can boost memory, clarify thoughts, fend off negativity, and block evil. Also known as a protector of women, this herb can be used to encourage faithful marriages. It can also increase luck when dealing with family matters. *USE: Add rosemary to love and financial abundance spells.*

Sage is an enforcer of positivity and it repels negative energies. It has the ability to purify the body. Sage is known to advance mental abilities, leading the way to obtain wisdom. It is believed to nurture all levels of health, including physical, spiritual, mental, and emotional. Some have even been known to use sage for immortality, longevity, and desired wishes. *USE: Add sage to mojo bags to enhance wisdom and clarity.*

Sandalwood is believed to be equivalent to the mind's eye and Root Chakra. Many people use it for exorcism, consecration, strong defense, and energies to heal. Its properties can enhance manifestation for those deep in reflection. Some people have used sandalwood to remain safe, bring peace, and remove and/or block negativity. *USE: Add sandalwood to an incense blend or burn it alone to remove negative energy and welcome good energy.*

Sea salt is a perfect anchor for those who need grounding. Many people gravitate to this ingredient for protective magick and rituals. It functions as a sponge by soaking up psychic energies. Sea salt acts as a representative for the Earth element because it is a product of the Earth's ground. Salt, mud, sand, stone, dirt, or anything that is used as ground represents the Earth element. Sea salt can also be used to cleanse crystals. Some will also use this wonderful ingredient for casting circles to cleanse, purify, or protect properties. A circle of salt keeps unwanted and negative forces out of the encircled area. Those who desire prosperity and abundance have been known to work with this ingredient too. *USE: Add a line of blessed sea salt along each doorway and window that has access to the outdoors to dispel negative energy from entering the building.*

Sugar was referred to as white gold once upon a time. This sweet ingredient emanates powerful attraction energies as many have used it in love matters. It is believed to be a strong enticer with sex magick for those who desire more. Many have said sugar can aid in struggling relationships that need work. *USE: Add sugar to a jar with a petition to sweeten another's intentions toward you.*

Thyme is a magnet of love and affection. It is known to keep a home full of joy and peace. Thyme can also be used to maintain good health within one's household. It amplifies positive vibrations and encourages good opinions. Many who seek loyalty will ensure thyme is there for their support. This is powerful enough to banish night terrors, which encourages tranquil sleep. It's also believed to build up a steady current of money if you desire a continuous flow. *USE: Add thyme to a spiritual bath to ensure a continuous flow of money.*

TOP EIGHT HERBS AND ROOTS FOR COMMON USES

Many herbs and roots have similar purposes when used in rituals and spells. If you have a specific intention you'd like to achieve, here are several common herbs and roots to choose from for each type of association.

CLEANSING AND PURIFICATION HERBS

Clove	Myrrh
Galangal root	Palo santo
Hyssop	Peppermint
Lavender	Sage

DISPELLING NEGATIVE ENERGY HERBS

Basil

Clove

Galangal root

Hyssop

Myrrh

Pepper

Sandalwood

Thyme

LOVE HERBS

Adam and Eve

Basil

Catnip

Cinnamon

Lavender

Lemon balm

Patchouli

Rose

LUCK HERBS

Basil

Chamomile

Clover

Five finger grass

High John the Conqueror

Lemon balm

Mustard seed

Peppermint

MONEY HERBS

Bay leaf

Cinnamon

Dill

Five finger grass

High John the Conqueror

Peppermint

Patchouli

Pine

PASSION HERBS

Basil	Dill
Catnip	Fennel seeds
Clove	Juniper berries
Coriander	Patchouli

PROSPERITY HERBS

Allspice	Ginger
Anise star pods	Linden
Bay leaf	Nutmeg
Chamomile	Orange peel

PROTECTION HERBS

Anise star pods	Linden
Basil	Myrrh
Dill	Parsley
Galangal root	Pepper

SUCCESS HERBS

Alfalfa	Five finger grass
Bergamot	Ginger
Cinnamon	High John the Conqueror
Clove	Mandrake

PSYCHIC AND SPIRITUAL DEVELOPMENT HERBS

Anise star pods

Bay leaf

Cinnamon

Frankincense

Lavender

Mugwort

Rose

Thyme

CHAPTER 4

FLOORWASHES AND CONJURE WATERS

In the rootwork tradition, it is necessary to keep your house and office clean and in order. Cleaning is a ritual used by rootworkers from the past and present to maintain the smooth flow of energy, attracting the positive. Every part of your home and office, including the doors, floors, walls, and windows needs a good cleaning. Once every area is free from dirt, dust, and residue, it'll be easier to maintain cleanliness throughout the year.

Before using any conjured waters, it is best to start with a clean home or office for cleansing and blessing rituals. The conjured waters are formulated with herbs, oils, and minerals to attract a goal toward you or dispel specific energies away from you. Choose a conjured water that is fresh, with the magickal and spiritual properties that best align with your intentions. Prepare your space with prayer, then wipe down and wash your entire area with the conjured water. This hoodoo tradition is the way to cleanse, bless, and be ready to manifest physically.

Many spiritual bath formulas found in the following chapter are helpful for conjured waters and floorwash formulas. Please review Chapter 5: Spiritual Baths to see other recipes that dispel negative energies and psychic attacks, drawing new love and money toward you.

Here are other ways to use conjured waters:

* Anoint people, places, or things
* Body sprays
* Spiritual baths
* Floorwashes
* Offerings
* Cleansing tonics (including altar spaces, amulets, candles, charms, mojo bags, objects, properties, talismans, and tools)

MATERIALS

It is best to use ingredients that are high-quality and organic, especially if any part of your body will emerge into an herbal blended formula. Also, please consider clean, filtered, and high-quality water that is free from harsh chemicals. Spring and distilled water are preferred.

HOLY WATER AND FLOORWASH FORMULA

Use the water as a floorwash to purify and bless your home.

3 teaspoons kosher sea salt

1 quart spring water

Pray over the ingredients and tools 23 times with Psalm 23 (see page 75). Pour the salt into the water. Then pour the mixture into a 1-quart glass jar.

PEACE WATER CONJURE FORMULA

Use this formula to bring about peace and maintain a well-balanced and harmonic vibe in your environment. Sprinkle the peace water on the four corners inside of your property. This may be used inside the home, particularly in a room you're renting. You may also anoint the windows and doors with this water. Use this formula once a month or as needed.

1 gallon distilled water

1 cup dried basil

1 cup dried hyssop

1 tablespoon Bay rum

Pray over your ingredients and tools. Any plea or mantra that comes from your heart commanding or asking for cleansing will work. Or you can use any mantra from a tradition that you connect with. Psalms 6, 23, 51, and 91 are also traditionally used. Boil equal parts water and herbs then simmer for 20 minutes in a nonaluminum pot over medium heat. Mix the herbs frequently with a wooden spoon to infuse the properties. Turn off the stove and add the Bay rum. Strain the herbs (or include the herbal mixture) and set aside two medium mixing bowls of the liquid for conjure water and floorwash. Once the mixture is room temperature, place it into a 1-gallon glass mason jar with a lid. Store the water in a well-controlled environment for seven days before using it.

ROSE WATER FLOORWASH FORMULA

This is a high vibrational water made with a very powerful flower—rose. Use this type of water for everyday rituals, especially for special love ceremonies and spells that draw new love to you or enhance your attraction. You can also use it as needed to maintain a loving and harmonious home. Rose has multiple uses that not only benefit you on a spiritual level but also improve your health and wellness. Using this formula can enhance your mood and put you in a calm state of mind.

12 roses

1 to 2 gallons distilled water

Pray over your ingredients and tools. Remove the rose petals from the stems and wash. Add the petals to a large nonaluminum pot. Cover the petals with the water then let simmer for 20 minutes over medium-low heat. Mix the petals frequently with the wooden spoon to infuse their properties. Turn off the stove. Strain the petals and set aside

2 medium mixing bowls of the liquid for conjure water and floorwash. Once the mixture is at room temperature, place it into a 2½-gallon ceramic, glass, or stainless steel jug and glass or stainless steel spray bottle. Place the containers in the refrigerator for up to 7 days to preserve the shelf life.

UNCROSSING CONJURE WATER FORMULA

This conjure water is used for an emergency, such as sudden disharmony in the home that reaches the point that you consider moving or temporarily leaving. Also, if you feel that your mind-body-soul connection is unbalanced or if you experience unwanted thoughts that aren't yours, clouding your mind due to someone playing a trick on you, then use this formula.

½ cup horseradish root powder

3 cups Holy Water Floorwash Formula (see page 63)

1 tablespoon white vinegar

Pray over your ingredients. Mix the ingredients together in a medium bowl using a wooden spoon, and add to a glass or stainless steel spray bottle. Starting from the farthest room in your house from the front and back doors, spray in the corners and windowsills. Spray any fireplaces and doors that lead outside. This will clear out any evil tricks cast upon you.

UNCROSSING AND GOOD LUCK FLOORWASH FORMULA

Use this floorwash for uncrossing and bringing good luck into your home. All you need is uncrossing water and van-van oil.

4 cups Uncrossing Conjure Water Formula (page 65)

½ cup van-van oil

Mix the two ingredients and wash all the floors in your home or business starting from the farthest room to the front door, including the outdoor porch, stairs, and walkways that lead to your home or business. Do this three times a week until you see a positive sign.

WAR WATER CONJURE FORMULA

This water formula is used to bring disharmony to an individual or household.

1 cup sea salt, divided

3 teaspoons Spanish moss

3 iron nails

3 honey black locust thorns

3 teaspoons white vinegar

1 pint thunderstorm or rainwater

1 teaspoon magnetic sand

Pray over your ingredients and tools. Add a teaspoon of salt, the Spanish moss, iron nails, and honey black locust thorns into 1-pint glass, ceramic, or stainless steel container and mix together using a wooden spoon to infuse the properties. Add all the liquid ingredients to a pint container, followed by the magnetic sand. Add the remaining salt to a sachet.

Upon arrival at the targeted individual's location, have the sachet of sea salt ready. Sprinkle salt on the ground with your left hand. Do this before you step onto the ground from the vehicle if you have driven to your destination. Continue to sprinkle sea salt along your path. Splash and pour the water formula into the walkway and the door entries of the targeted individual. Once you complete this, turn around and do not look back. Throw sea salt across your left shoulder with your right hand while sprinkling salt along your path with your left hand as you return to your vehicle. Once home, take a purification bath.

CRYSTAL CHARGED CONJURE WATER FORMULA

Use this formula to cleanse and charge tools and ingredients or for conjure waters, floorwashes, or other rituals and spells.

1 clear quartz

1 gallon spring water

Place the quartz into a 1-gallon glass jar filled with water. Place the jar in a safe area outside to receive the moonlight of a full moon. Remove the jar before sunrise and place it in a dark area within the home. Place the jar back outside to receive the moonlight of the full moon on the second night. Again, remove the jar before sunrise and place in a dark area. On the third night place a jar outside once again to receive the moonlight of the full moon. Then remove the jar before sunrise and place in a dark area. Once the sun sets, the water is ready for use.

FLORIDA WATER

Some waters are used in hoodoo to make very powerful colognes. Other magickal and spiritual practices may also use them for blessing, cleansing, healing, and offerings. Florida water (known as "flowery" and not after the Southern state) is well-known worldwide and will be the main focus of a water and alcohol-based cologne. You can buy this type of spiritual cologne, but if, like me, you find making your own formulas empowering and ancestor-led, consider making your own.

½ cup dried cedarwood	½ cup dried lemongrass
9 cinnamon sticks	½ cup whole cloves
½ cup dried lavender buds	½ gallon vodka
½ cup dried lemon peels	½ gallon distilled water

Pray over your ingredients and tools. Add all of the herbs and flowers to a 2½-gallon ceramic, glass, or stainless steel jug with dispenser. Pour the alcohol into the mixture, then add the distilled water and close the lid. Place the jug in a dark area for 20 days.

On the fifth and twentieth days, observe the formula and gently mix herbal blends. On the twentieth day, dispense the liquid from the jug. If your jug does not have a dispenser, strain the herbs and set them aside for reserves. Add Florida water into a glass or stainless steel spray bottle for immediate use. Use within 12 weeks. You may use this formula as a floorwash or add it to your other floorwash formulas. Do this at least once a month or as needed.

DRAWING MONEY AND GOOD LUCK FLOORWASH FORMULA

Use this floorwash to draw in quick money and good luck. Wash all the floors in your home or business, starting with the room that is farthest from the front door. Include the outdoor porch, stairs, and outdoor walkways that lead to your home or business. Do this at least once a month or as needed.

¼ cup vodka

⅛ cup dried basil

½ quart distilled water

⅛ cup dried lavender buds

⅛ cup dried peppermint leaves

⅛ cup dried pine needles

⅛ cup dried rosemary

Pray over your ingredients and tools. Add all of the ingredients to a nonaluminum pot and bring to a boil. Let simmer for 20 minutes. Mix the herbs frequently to infuse their properties. Strain the herbs and set them aside to use as desired. Once the mixture is at room temperature, place it into a 1-quart ceramic, glass, or stainless steel container. Store the water in a well-controlled environment for seven days before using it.

PROSPERITY AND SUCCESS FLOORWASH FORMULA

Use this floorwash for prosperity and success. Wash all the floors in your home or business, starting with the room that is farthest from the front door. Include the outdoor porch, stairs, and outdoor walkways that lead to your home or business. Do this at least once a month or as needed.

⅛ cup dried bay leaves

¼ cup Florida water
(see page 68)

⅛ cup dried patchouli leaves

⅛ cup dried peppermint
leaves

Pray over your ingredients and tools. Add all of the ingredients to a nonaluminum pot and bring to a boil. Let simmer for 20 minutes. Mix the herbs frequently with a wooden spoon to infuse their properties. Strain the herbs and set them aside to use as desired. Once the mixture is at room temperature, place it into a 1-quart container. Store the water in a well-controlled environment for seven days before using it.

EMPLOYMENT AND BUSINESS GOOD LUCK FLOORWASH FORMULA

Use this floorwash for employment and business luck. Wash all the floors in your home or business, starting from the room that is farthest from the front door. Include the outdoor porch, stairs, and outdoor walkways that lead to your home or business. Do this at least once a month or as needed.

¼ cup vodka

⅛ cup dried cinnamon
powder

1 quart distilled water

⅛ cup dried
peppermint leaves

⅛ cup dried rosemary

⅛ cup dried sage

9 sugar cubes

⅛ cup dried sweet basil

Pray over your ingredients and tools. Add all of the ingredients to a nonaluminum pot and bring to a boil. Let simmer for 20 minutes. Mix the herbs frequently with a wooden spoon to infuse their properties. Strain the herbs and set them aside to use as desired. Once the mixture is at room temperature, place it into a 1-quart container. Store the water in a well-controlled environment for seven days before using it.

RAINWATER RITUAL

Rainwater is a powerful ingredient for cleansing, healing, and charging. Use it straight from the source or blend it with herbs and oils for a variety of purposes. Here are some ideas for using rainwater:

* Gather the first rainfall of the season for purification ritual. Use water for handwashing rituals, offerings, and cleansing rituals.

  * Tip: To gather rainwater, look up the weather ahead of time to know when it will next rain. Leave a bucket, cup, or large bowl outside to collect the water.

* Gather thunderstorm rain for charging purposes. This type of rainfall is very powerful. Use this water to charge conjure waters, floorwashes, tools, talisman, amulets, crystals, and ritual ingredients.

* Make a rainwater money wash. Wash your money with rainwater to protect your investments.

CHAPTER 5

※

SPIRITUAL BATHS

※

Water is one of the most important elements in our world. It is one of the main sources of all life. All creatures, including human beings and animals, depend on this precious resource for survival. Did you know that the human body has a very high percentage of water? Our skin, the largest organ that is visible to our eyes, also contains water. Think about your brain, heart, lungs, muscles, and other internal organs. They all contain water.

Water encompasses the past, the present, and the future. This element is holy and existed beyond our time. Water plays a significant role in rootwork. The reason why I mentioned the skin is because soaking in water is essential to the practice. Your personal purity is not only necessary for the success of your rituals and spells but also for your spiritual and personal developmental growth. The spiritual baths that you soak in are used for spiritual cleansing, protecting, blessing, and attracting specific goals toward you. The main goal for your spiritual bath will purify your body, uplift your mind, and refresh your spirit. During this time, your physical and energetic being comes into alignment and vibrates at a higher level.

Spiritual baths consist of herbal blends. Each blend consists of fresh or dried herbs, oils, minerals, and any other necessary ingredient to help manifest your needs. This ritual is sacred, just as water is sacred. Water is not only magickal but a powerful and valuable healing ingredient that shouldn't be overlooked or treated with disregard. There are millions in this world who do not have access to clean water, so pray and treat this water and any water ritual with utmost respect.

This chapter includes many bath formulas for different purposes, including dispelling negativity, cleansing the energetic field of your body, emotional clearing, and welcoming the energies of your desires toward you.

BLESSING SPIRITUAL BATHS AND WATERS

My family taught me to always pray over my ingredients. Growing up, I also saw this type of consecrating preparation in religious and spiritual practice. I attended a Catholic school from kindergarten up until high school. Attending church to pray and light candles was ordinary during school. It was also similar to what I did at home. Since the age of five, I have loved the rituals, chants, and songs. I was determined to learn what the nuns and priests knew. I was a very curious and open-minded child who loved to learn about spirituality. The only way I was able to learn the hidden knowledge was to be baptized with holy water by the priest. I remember it like it was yesterday. It was a Holy Saturday of my fifth-grade year and I, along with two adults, wore brown gowns with a rope belt tied around my waist. I walked down the church aisle to stand before a small kiddie pool. The church was packed with people sitting in every pew. I sat in the middle of the pool as the priest blessed and poured holy water over my head and body. After that spiritual cleanse and baptism into another faith, my spiritual growth continued to increase.

I decided to become an altar server with my mom. I felt blessed to have had sacred responsibilities alongside her. During those times, I witnessed numerous acts of the priest consecrating over holy water, incense, rosaries, and more. I took on the task of holding the holy water during special ceremonies while the priest dipped the water tool and used it to bless the congregation as we walked around. Sister Maria was a mentor of mine at the time. One day she asked me to attend church to have my feet washed by the priest along with others. I was honored and had my feet washed with holy water and blessed before the congregation.

I share this particular experience because a spiritual bath can be done in various ways, especially if you do not have a bathtub. You can use a bowl and pour the spiritual water formula over your head or body or sprinkle it over you. You can also submerge your feet in a bowl of the formula for a period of time. Do what comes naturally and easily when preparing to give yourself a spiritual bath.

Remember, to pray over the ingredients that you choose. If you have a calling to say your own prayer or a prayer that intuitively comes to you, say it. Or take some time to write out a special prayer for consecration. I recite what comes intuitively, and if I have a calling to recite a family tradition, I recite the Psalm 23 verse. This verse has been a family tradition from both my African and Filipino lineage for many generations, and I share it with you to recite if you have a connection to do so.

PSALM 23

Recite PSALM 23 while preparing your ingredients and spiritual bath ritual.

The Lord is my shepherd; I shall not want.

He maketh me to lie down in green pastures.

He leadeth me beside the still waters.

He restoreth my soul.

*He leadeth me in the paths of
righteousness for His name's sake.*

*Yea, though I walk through the valley
of the shadow of death,*

I will fear no evil for thou art with me.

Thy rod and Thy staff they comfort me.

*Thou preparest a table before me in
the presence of mine enemies.*

Thou anointest my head with oil.

My cup runneth over.

*Surely goodness and mercy shall follow
me all the days of my life,*

And I will dwell in the house of the Lord forever. Amen.

MATERIALS

You must be prepared with all the required ingredients prior to engaging in any type of ritual. It is best to use ingredients that are high-quality and organic, especially if any part of your body will emerge into an herbal blended formula. Also, please consider clean, filtered, and high-quality water that is free from harsh chemicals. Spring and alkaline water are preferred.

HERBS

Place dried herbs and roots in a muslin bag, then place the bag directly inside the water or tie it to the faucet as the water is running. You may place fresh herbs and roots inside a muslin bag as well or place them directly into the bath. Be sure to gather the herbs for disposal before draining the water. Store your freshly picked or dried herbs in a glass jar with water and keep them in a dark area to preserve the active properties. Use within a few days.

SALTS AND BAKING SODAS

Each formula that includes salts will yield at least 3 cups total for future baths or sharing with others, unless otherwise stated. Add 1 cup of the formula to your bath. Store the rest in a container for future use. Keep in a cool, dry place for up to 3 months.. Epsom salt, coarse sea salt, and baking soda are the best ingredients to work with.

Types of salt:

* Dead Sea salt
* Epsom salt
* Himalayan salt
* Kosher rock salt
* Sea salt

ESSENTIAL OILS

Always mix essential oils with a carrier oil for bath formulas. Essential oils may not dissolve into the water easily. Mixing it into a carrier oil first will allow the oil to be dispersed into the water properly. Use only 5 to 8 drops of essential oil in ½ ounce of carrier oil or 1 ounce of bath salts for your bath formulas. If you do not have a carrier oil, the other option is to use a dropper and disperse 5 to 8 drops of essential oils into the water. Use amber or dark-colored jars and bottles for mixtures that include essential oils to preserve the quality.

Types of essential oils:

* Basil
* Bergamot
* Cedarwood
* Cinnamon
* Clove
* Frankincense
* Geranium
* Jasmine
* Lavender
* Nutmeg
* Patchouli
* Peppermint
* Rose
* Rosemary
* Sandalwood
* Ylang-ylang

Types of carrier oils:

* Apricot kernel
* Avocado
* Coconut
* Jojoba
* Olive (extra virgin)
* Sesame
* Sweet almond

COOKWARE

Use only cast-iron, ceramic, glass, porcelain, or stainless-steel cookware to steep your herbs. Please avoid using aluminum cookware. Soak your herbs in cold to room-temperature water for 20 minutes, then place on the stove and bring to a gentle boil. Next, reduce the heat and let your ingredients simmer for 20 minutes. Remove the cookware from the heat and strain the herbs. Allow some time to cool down before pouring the herbal liquid blend into a suitable container. Store away from direct sunlight.

OTHER MATERIALS

* Amber bottles or jars
* Cutting board
* Dropper
* Edible flowers
* Foldable and portable bathtub (optional)
* Food scale
* Foot spa tub
* Glass containers
* Labels
* Mason jars: gallon (128 oz.), liter (33.8 oz.), quart (32 oz.), pint (16 oz.), half pint (8 oz.), and quarter pint (4 oz.)

- ❋ Measuring cups
- ❋ Measuring spoons
- ❋ Minerals (organic)
- ❋ Mixing bowls (glass, wooden, or stainless steel)

- ❋ Mortar and pestle
- ❋ Muslin bags
- ❋ Strainer
- ❋ Spices
- ❋ Spoons

PRECAUTIONS AND SAFETY MEASURES

Consider your safety and well-being. Take precautions seriously. Not all essential oils, carrier oils, herbs, salts, and water temperatures are acceptable for pregnancy, nursing, those trying to conceive, children, people with allergies, those taking medications, and the like. Please remain under the supervision of a qualified health-care practitioner should you decide to use any ingredients that you do not normally use. Consult with a health-care provider that is knowledgeable on herbalism and aromatherapy to let you know if specific herbs or oils are acceptable for you to use based on your own health situation. It is vital to have a trusting relationship with your health-care providers because they are trained and there to serve you whenever it is required.

SPIRITUAL BATH FORMULAS FOR CLEANSING AND PURIFYING

Regularly maintaining positive aura and energy is important for your body and health. Use these formulas to remove any negative energies or spirits.

THE HOLY FORMULA

This bath formula helps remove all forms of uncleanness.

   1 tablespoon hyssop

   1 quart purified water

Pray over your ingredients and tools. Boil equal parts of water and herbs for 20 minutes in a nonaluminum pot. Mix the herbs frequently to infuse their properties. Strain the herbs. Once the liquid mixture is at room temperature, place it into a glass jar. Use the liquid for your bath and pour it over your head three times as you pray. Soak and relax for at least 20 minutes. Do this at least once a month or as needed.

THE 13-DAY SPIRITUAL BATH FORMULA

The 13-Day Spiritual Bath Formula is used to cleanse, remove bad luck, and expel curses and negative energies. Thirteen herbs and roots are used in this formula. If you are unable to find any of these ingredients, view Chapter 3, Herbs and Roots, for possible substitutions.

Angelica root	Mint
Basil	Patchouli
Bay leaves	Peppermint
Cedarwood	Rosemary
Hyssop	Sage
Lavender buds	Sandalwood
Lemon verbena	

Pray over your ingredients and tools. Boil equal parts of water and herbs for 30 minutes in a nonaluminum pot. Mix the herbal concoction frequently to infuse the properties. Strain the herbs and set aside a bowl of the liquid for your bath. Use the liquid for your bath and pour it over your head 13 times. Soak and relax for 13 minutes. You will do this for 13 consecutive days to achieve a successful spiritual bath cleanse.

THE PROTECTION SPIRITUAL BATH

This rejuvenating bath will leave you feeling relaxed and supple.

2 tablespoons Dead Sea salt

3 drops lavender essential oil

1 ounce carrier oil
(apricot kernel, olive oil,
or sweet almond oil)

1 tablespoon rosemary
(dried or fresh)

1 tablespoon sage leaves
(dried or fresh)

Pray over your ingredients and tools. Add all of the ingredients to a bowl and mix thoroughly. Add the formula to your spiritual bath. Pour the bathwater over your head three times. Soak and relax for 20 minutes. Once you're done, safely remove and discard the herbs from the bath. Repeat the bath as needed.

PURIFICATION SPIRITUAL BATH

This bath formula will help cleanse your chakras and aura and clear your mind.

½ cup baking soda

3 cups Epsom salt (alternatively, use kosher rock salt)

½ cup Pink Himalayan salt (alternatively, use coarse sea salt)

5 drops frankincense essential oil

5 drops lavender essential oil

1 ounce carrier oil of choice

1 tablespoon rosemary (dried or fresh)

Pray over your ingredients and tools. Add the baking soda, Epsom salt, and Himalayan salt to a bowl. Next, add the frankincense and lavender essential oil. Then, add the carrier oil of your choice. Mix thoroughly. Add the dried or fresh rosemary to the mixture. Add 1 cup of the formula to your spiritual bath. Pour the bathwater over your head three times. Soak and relax for 20 minutes. After your bath, remove and discard the herbs from the bath safely. Repeat the bath as needed.

THE 7-DAY CLEANSING SPIRITUAL BATH

Similar to the 13-Day Spiritual Bath Formula, this bath will rid you of negative blockages and energies and bad luck.

3 cups baking soda

1½ cups Pink Himalayan salt

Pray over your ingredients and tools. Add the baking soda and Himalayan salt to a bowl. Mix thoroughly. Add 1 cup of the formula to your spiritual bath. Pour the bathwater over your head three times. Soak and relax for 20 minutes. Repeat for seven consecutive days.

PROTECTION FROM PSYCHIC ATTACKS SPIRITUAL BATH

This bath formula helps guard you against any hexes.

1 ounce carrier oil of choice

10 drops cedarwood essential oil

Pray over your ingredients and tools. Add the oils to a bowl. Mix thoroughly. Add the formula to your spiritual bath. Pour the bathwater over your head three times. Soak and relax for 20 minutes. Repeat for three consecutive days.

Recite: "Please assist in releasing me from an energetics field and return me to the light" as you pray over your tools, while you pour the bathwater over your head, and while you soak to maintain your intent throughout the ritual.

REMOVE BLOCKS SPIRITUAL BATH

This bath formula helps promote clarity, certainty, and spiritual growth.

5 drops lavender essential oil

5 drops lemon essential oil

1 ounce carrier oil of choice

½ cup lavender buds (dried or fresh)

½ cup lemon peels

1 cup fresh peppermint leaves

3 cinnamon sticks

Pray over your ingredients and tools. Add the essential oils to a bowl. Then add your carrier oil. Mix thoroughly. Add the lavender buds, lemon peels, and peppermint leaves. Add the formula and the cinnamon to your spiritual bath. Pour the bathwater over your head three times. Soak and relax for 20 minutes. Once you're done, remove and discard the herbs and cinnamon sticks from the bath safely. Repeat the bath as needed.

THE HEALING SPIRITUAL BATH

This bath heals and resets your energy, emotional balance, and mental clarity, relaxing you and putting you at ease.

1 cup rosemary (dried or fresh)

1 cup of sage leaves (dried or fresh)

1 cup thyme leaves (dried or fresh)

Pray over your ingredients and tools. Add all of the herbs to a bowl. Mix thoroughly, then add the formula to your spiritual bath or place it inside a muslin bag to keep the herbs together. Pour the bathwater over your head three times. Soak and relax for 20 minutes. Once you're done, safely remove and discard the herbs from the bath. Repeat the bath as needed.

SPIRITUAL BATHS FOR MATTERS OF LOVE

Whether you're looking to attract new love, increase friendships, or manifest a specific desire, these formulas will help amplify all areas of love in your life.

THE APHRODISIAC SPIRITUAL BATH

This spiritual bath is excellent for promoting your charm, your sensuality, and your sexual energy.

5 drops jasmine essential oil

5 drops sandalwood essential oil

3 drops ylang-ylang essential oil

1 ounce sweet almond carrier oil

1 cup rose petals (dried or fresh)

Pray over your ingredients and tools. Add the essential oils to a bowl, followed by the carrier oil. Mix thoroughly. Add the formula along with the rose petals to your spiritual bath. Pour the bathwater over your head five times. Soak and relax for 20 minutes. Once you're done, remove and discard the petals from the bath safely. Repeat the bath as needed.

THE FERTILITY SPIRITUAL BATH

This spiritual bath formula promotes and increases your libido, the potency of sperm, and your chances of getting pregnant.

- 1 ounce carrier oil of choice
- 10 drops rose essential oil
- 1 cup rose petals (dried or fresh)

Pray over your ingredients and tools. Add the oils to a bowl and mix thoroughly. Add the formula along with the rose petals to your spiritual bath. Pour the bathwater over your head five times. Soak and relax for 20 minutes. Repeat as needed and only when you are not ovulating.

Recite or use a prayer that matches your intentions for trying to conceive or for a healthy and spiritual reproductive system that is ready to allow your future babies to grow.

THE NEW LOVE SPIRITUAL BATH

This spiritual formula is great for attracting new love toward you.

- ½ cup baking soda
- 3 cups Epsom salt (alternatively, use kosher rock salt)
- ½ cup Pink Himalayan salt (alternatively, use coarse sea salt)
- 5 drops cinnamon essential oil
- 5 drops lavender essential oil

5 drops rose essential oil

1 ounce carrier oil of choice

1 cup rose petals
(dried or fresh)

Pray over your ingredients and tools. Add the baking soda, Epsom salt, and Pink Himalayan salt to a bowl. Add the essential oils, followed by the carrier oil. Mix thoroughly. Add 1 cup of the formula plus the rose petals to your spiritual bath. Pour the bathwater over your head five times. Soak and relax for 20 minutes. Once you're done, remove and discard the flowers from the bath safely. Repeat the bath on Mondays and Saturdays as needed or once on a full moon.

Recite a prayer while making the formula and during the bath to strengthen your intent and concentrate on your new love intentions and desires.

THE ATTRACTION SPIRITUAL BATH

Use this spiritual bath formula to attract your desires toward you.

½ cup baking soda

3 cups Epsom salt
(alternatively, use
kosher rock salt)

½ cup Pink Himalayan
salt (alternatively, use
coarse sea salt)

5 drops bergamot
essential oil

5 drops cinnamon
essential oil

5 drops patchouli
essential oil

1 ounce carrier oil of choice

1 cup rose petals

Pray over you ingredients and tools. Add the baking soda, Epsom salt, and Pink Himalayan salt to a bowl. Add the essential oils, followed by the carrier oil. Mix thoroughly. Add 1 cup of formula plus the rose petals to your spiritual bath. Pour the bathwater over your head five times. Soak and relax for 20 minutes. Once you're done, remove and discard the flowers from the bath safely. Repeat the bath for three consecutive days or once on a full moon.

Recite a prayer and concentrate on your intentions and desires toward you.

SPIRITUAL BATH FORMULAS FOR FINANCIAL INCREASE

Use these spiritual bath formulas to help increase abundance and prosperity in your life.

THE EMPLOYMENT MAGNET SPIRITUAL BATH

This spiritual bath is for all matters related to employment, including good luck with application submissions, interviews, promotions, positive reviews, etc.

½ cup baking soda

3 cups Epsom salt (alternatively, use kosher rock salt)

½ cup Pink Himalayan salt (alternatively, use coarse sea salt)

5 drops cinnamon essential oil

5 drops geranium
essential oil

5 drops peppermint
essential oil

1 ounce carrier oil of choice

1 tablespoon rosemary
(dried or fresh)

Pray over your ingredients and tools. Add the baking soda, Epsom salt, and Pink Himalayan salt to a bowl. Add the essential oils, followed by the carrier oil. Mix thoroughly. Add the rosemary to the mixture. Add 1 cup of the formula to your spiritual bath. Pour the bathwater over your head seven times. Soak and relax for 20 minutes. Once you're done, safely remove and discard the herbs from the bath. Repeat the bath as needed on Thursdays.

Recite Psalm 23 or concentrate on your employment intentions and desires.

THE PROSPERITY SPIRITUAL BATH

This spiritual bath formula is for attracting prosperity toward you.

½ cup baking soda

3 cups Epsom salt
(alternatively, use
kosher rock salt)

½ cup Pink Himalayan
salt (alternatively, use
coarse sea salt)

5 drops cinnamon
essential oil

5 drops nutmeg essential oil

5 drops sandalwood
essential oil

1 ounce carrier oil of choice

Pray over your ingredients and tools. Add the baking soda, Epsom salt, and Pink Himalayan salt to a bowl. Add the essential oils, followed by the carrier oil. Mix thoroughly. Add 1 cup of the formula to your spiritual bath. Pour the bathwater over your head seven times. Soak and relax for 20 minutes. Once you're done, safely remove and discard the herbs from the bath. Repeat the bath for three consecutive days starting on a full moon.

Recite a prayer and concentrate on your prosperity intentions and desires.

GOOD LUCK SPIRITUAL BATH

This spiritual bath formula is for good luck with gambling and lottery games.

½ cup baking soda

3 cups Epsom salt (alternatively, use kosher rock salt)

½ cup Pink Himalayan salt (alternatively, use coarse sea salt)

5 drops basil essential oil

5 drops cedarwood essential oil

5 drops clove essential oil

5 drops nutmeg essential oil

5 drops sage essential oil

1 ounce carrier oil of choice

½ cup chamomile flowers (dried)

Pray over your ingredients and tools. Add the baking soda, Epsom salt, and Pink Himalayan salt to a bowl. Add the essential oils, followed by the carrier oil. Mix thoroughly. Add 1 cup of the formula along with the chamomile flowers to your spiritual bath. Pour the bathwater over your head seven times. Soak and relax for 20 minutes. Once you're done, remove and discard the flowers from the bath safely. Repeat the bath for three consecutive days starting on a full moon.

Recite a prayer and concentrate on your good luck intentions and desires to win.

MONEY-DRAWING SPIRITUAL BATH

This spiritual bath formula is for all matters pertaining to money drawing.

½ cup baking soda

3 cups Epsom salt (alternatively, use kosher rock salt)

½ cup Pink Himalayan salt (alternatively, use coarse sea salt)

5 drops cinnamon essential oil

5 drops nutmeg essential oil

5 drops peppermint essential oil

1 ounce carrier oil of choice

¼ cup lavender buds (dried)

Pray over your ingredients and tools. Add the baking soda, Epsom salt, and Pink Himalayan salt to a bowl. Add the essential oils, followed by the carrier oil. Mix thoroughly. Add 1 cup of the formula along with the lavender buds to your spiritual bath. Pour the bathwater over your head seven times. Soak and relax for 20 minutes. Once you're done, remove and discard the flowers from the bath safely. Repeat the bath on Thursdays and Sundays as needed, or once on a full moon.

THE LITTLE BOOK OF ROOTWORK

Recite a prayer and concentrate on your money-drawing intentions and desires.

CHAPTER 6

---- ✳ ----

INCENSE

---- ✳ ----

For many centuries, incense has been a main staple for medicinal healing, prayer, and sacred ceremonial work all around the world. In rootwork, incense has many purposes with assisting magickal and spiritual rituals. There are four primary purposes in using incense in rootwork.

* The first purpose is to purify an object, person, or place. Using incense for purification can dispel unwanted and stagnant energies.

* The second purpose is to manifest. Similar to setting your intentions with candle magick, speak or write down your intentions for a specific goal and allow the burning session to attract it back toward you. For example, if your goal is to attract your soulmate, you would use incense to attract love and a new relationship.

* The third purpose is for prayer. The smoke is said to help send prayers to the ancestors, God, and spirit guides. As you burn your incense, you are either in meditation, concentrating on your prayers, reciting a series of invocations, or simply being present and allowing your inner thoughts to speak your words of worship.

* Lastly, the fourth purpose is for offerings. You can burn a specific incense as an offering of honor and respect to your ancestors, spirit guides, or other deities for your rituals and spells. There's an equal exchange of giving and receiving.

TYPES OF INCENSE

There are several forms of incense: cones, powder, resin, and sticks. Incense is made with dried herbs, flowers, roots, wood, resin, and other natural ingredients. You will easily find all types of incense at your local botanica, health food store, new age store, online shops, and even regular stores. Since you will be handling and inhaling the incense, it is best to use one made with high-quality, natural ingredients without synthetic and toxic chemicals.

USING AND CHOOSING INCENSE

For all types of incense, use only heat-resistant containers and holders. Incense sticks need a safe and secure holder to prevent any fire hazards. Incense cones, powder, and resin need to fit securely inside a heat-resistant container such as a cauldron, incense burner, or kettle. Never burn the incense out of sight. It is always best to burn it in a well-ventilated space.

In my family tradition, we use various Asian incense, especially ones made in India that utilize two powerful ingredients—patchouli and sandalwood—which give off an aromatic scent that you'll never forget. Any incense that uses patchouli as a main ingredient is always my all-time favorite to work with in rituals. It not only attracts your goals and desires but is a wonderful scent for meditation and personal development work as well.

The other types of incense that I love to use are found in Native American practices, including cedarwood, pine, and sage. These are my go-to ingredients for rituals pertaining to cleansing, blessing, and purifying. The scent of all three immediately brings a grounding effect to your body, mind, spirit, and soul connection. You can find these herbs in various incense types, but the most popular are bundles and individual sticks for smudging rituals.

Palo santo is a sacred wood from South America that has both powerful medicinal and spiritual properties. Similar to cedarwood, Palo Santo's scent is strong yet pleasantly earthy. The scent will help shift your mood and ground you to the earth. Palo Santo comes in various types of incense, but my favorite is the individual stick form.

I have the fondest memories from my childhood using incense at school. I attended a private Catholic school where incense played a major role during prayer time. The type of incense we used was resin. In the rootwork tradition, incense was used for sending our prayers to God. When I was eleven years old, I chose the path of becoming an altar server. Incense was essential to the rituals at school and church. I always looked forward to any special ceremonies that required us to help with holding the hanging incense burner that contained frankincense, myrrh, or sandalwood resin. My responsibility was to help the priest or nun in going around to purify the congregation, church, and property with the incense. Funerals were another special ceremony that required the use of incense at the church. During these ceremonies, we used incense's natural healing abilities to shift and affect the environment. As an herb, incense cleanses the atmosphere and adds energies into the environment. Incense promotes feelings within its users and allows people to go into trance states and higher states of consciousness.

When you choose an incense to work with based on your intentions, make sure you like the aromatic scent as well. This is very important and will help you focus on your rituals and spells more effectively. Should you desire to make your own incense, always pray over your ingredients and tools.

HOW TO BURN INCENSE

To light an incense stick, use a lighter or match, or place it over any open flame, let it catch fire, then quickly blow it out. The incense stick is ready to burn once you see that the tip of the stick is glowing ember red and is beginning to produce ash.

For resin incense, there are a couple of different methods of burning. A common method to burn resin incense is to get an incense burner or a censer, place an ignited charcoal briquette inside, wait for the briquette to turn ash gray, then place the resin on top. This creates a lot of smoke, so it's best to do this outside, in a garage, or in a well-ventilated area. Another way to burn resin is to get a wax warmer or a tealight burner, place a metal disk or aluminum foil over the top, and light a tealight candle underneath. Place the resin in the disk or aluminum and the resin will begin to melt and burn slowly. This method produces virtually no smoke and a light smell.

MATERIALS

This chapter includes my favorite incense formulas. All require the following:

Essential supplies:

* baking pan
* containers (preferably ceramic, glass, or stainless steel) with lids
* measuring spoons
* mixing bowls
* heat-resistant container
* hot charcoal block. The top places to purchase charcoal blocks are from botanicas, health food stores, new age stores, religious stores, and online.
* powders

Essential oils:

Suppose you are interested in making incense cones or sticks; I have a quick and easy way to speed up the process. You may purchase unscented incense cones or sticks in bulk online or in my shop. You will substitute any herbal powder ingredients for the high-quality essential oils of that type. For example, if a powder incense formula asks for peppermint herb in powdered form, you will substitute for 100 percent pure peppermint essential oil. Remember to use high-quality essential oils only. Another tip for making incense cones and sticks is to prepare your ingredients beforehand. You also want to ensure that you have enough essential oils to distribute the amounts correctly. Each incense should have at least 20 drops of essential oils in total.

INCENSE CONES AND STICKS

Premade unscented incense cones or sticks

Olive dish

Essential oils of choice

Drying container

Lay the unscented incense cone or stick on olive dish. Add a maximum of 20 drops of essential oil to cone or stick, allowing each droplet to spread evenly. Then rub the cone or stick onto the extra oil inside the olive dish. Coat it very well, then place the cone on a clean plate to dry for at least 24 hours. If you are using a stick, place it in an upright drying container such as a tall glass, tray, or vase to allow for at least 24 hours. After 24 hours, check the incense before burning.

The following incense formulas are for incense in the form of powder. Allow 24 to 72 hours to dry if the formula includes essential oils.

MONEY-DRAWING INCENSE

Cinnamon taps into the flow of plentitude. Burn this incense to attract prosperity and wealth to your home.

1 tablespoon cedarwood powder

3 tablespoons cinnamon powder

| 1 tablespoon High John the Conqueror root powder | 2 tablespoons peppermint powder |

Mix all of the ingredients together in a mixing bowl. Pour the formula into a container and cover. When you are ready to use it, measure one teaspoon of incense and place it on top of a hot charcoal block.

GOOD LUCK INCENSE

Bergamot and cedarwood attract prosperity, nutmeg and lemon are especially potent when used in combination, and High John the Conqueror brings a range of good luck elements.

20 drops bergamot essential oil	2 tablespoons cinnamon powder
5 drops clover essential oil	3 tablespoons High John the Conqueror root powder
10 drops lemon essential oil	
1 tablespoon cedarwood powder	1 tablespoon nutmeg powder

Mix all of the liquid ingredients together in a mixing bowl. Mix all of the powder ingredients together in another mixing bowl. Slowly pour the dry ingredients into the liquid mixing bowl and stir. Transfer the formula to a baking pan and spread it evenly. Allow the formula to dry for 1 hour, then transfer it into a container, cover with the lid, and gently shake to mix. When you are ready to use it, measure 1 teaspoon and place it on top of a hot charcoal block.

BUSINESS AND EMPLOYMENT SUCCESS INCENSE

The combination of essential oils and herbs in this incense will generate positive money vibes and open up a path of prosperity in business.

10 drops bergamot essential oil

5 drops clover essential oil

20 drops lavender essential oil

1 tablespoon cedarwood powder

2 tablespoons cinnamon powder

3 tablespoons High John the Conqueror Root powder

1 tablespoon nutmeg powder

Mix all of the liquid ingredients together in a mixing bowl. Mix all of the powder ingredients together in another mixing bowl. Slowly pour the dry ingredients into the liquid mixing bowl and stir. Transfer the formula to a baking pan and spread it evenly. Allow the formula to dry for 1 hour. Transfer the formula into a container, cover with the lid, and gently shake to mix. When you are ready to use it, measure 1 teaspoon and place on top of a hot charcoal block.

COME TO ME NOW INCENSE

This incense charms and commands the person of your choice to come to you. This can be a friend, a lover, an ex, a boss, or even a relative. Burn it at an altar or attempt to douse yourself in the smoke by wafting it toward you with your hand from your head to your feet. Keep your mind clear on your intentions.

1 tablespoon brown sugar

1 tablespoon catnip powder

3 tablespoons
cinnamon powder

1 tablespoon nutmeg powder

1 tablespoon rose powder

Mix all of the ingredients together in a mixing bowl. Pour the formula into a container with the lid. When you are ready to use it, measure 1 teaspoon of the formula and place it on top of a hot charcoal block.

LOVE-DRAWING INCENSE

Waft the smoke of this incense toward you to attract new love or friendship into your life. Burn it at your love altar or in any room of your home.

20 drops orange essential oil

20 drops patchouli
essential oil

3 tablespoons
cinnamon powder

1 tablespoon
coriander powder

1 tablespoon lemon
balm powder

1 tablespoon linden powder

1 tablespoon rose powder

Mix all of the liquid ingredients together in a mixing bowl. Mix all of the powder ingredients together in another mixing bowl. Slowly pour the dry ingredients into the liquid mixing bowl and stir. Transfer the formula to a baking pan and spread it evenly. Allow the formula to dry for 1 hour. Transfer the formula to a container, cover with the lid, and gently shake to mix. When you are ready to use it, measure 1 teaspoon of the formula and place it on top of a hot charcoal block.

INCREASE ATTRACTION AND LOVE INCENSE

Rose essential oil embodies love and promotes joy and relaxation. Combine it with frankincense, star anise, and cinnamon to spice up your love life.

20 drops frankincense essential oil

10 drops rose essential oil

1 tablespoon anise star powder

3 tablespoons cinnamon powder

2 tablespoons nutmeg powder

1 tablespoon sandalwood

Mix all of the liquid ingredients together in a mixing bowl. Mix all of the powder ingredients together in another mixing bowl. Slowly pour the dry ingredients into the liquid mixing bowl and stir. Transfer the formula to a baking pan and spread it evenly. Allow the formula to dry for 1 hour. Transfer the formula to a container, cover with a lid, and gently shake to mix. When you are ready to use it, measure 1 teaspoon of the formula and place it on top of a hot charcoal block.

MARRIAGE AND RELATIONSHIPS INCENSE

Strengthen your marriage bond with this powerful combination of stress-fighting patchouli essential oil, love-promoting rose essential oil, and a combination of herbal powders, including the powerful Adam and Eve powder, known for rekindling the flames of marriage.

10 drops patchouli essential oil

10 drops rose essential oil

1 tablespoon Adam and Eve powder

3 tablespoons cinnamon powder

1 tablespoon comfrey powder

1 tablespoon coriander powder

1 tablespoon rosemary powder

Mix all of the liquid ingredients together in a mixing bowl. Mix all of the powder ingredients together in another mixing bowl. Slowly pour the dry ingredients into the liquid mixing bowl and stir. Transfer the formula to a baking pan and spread it evenly. Allow the formula to dry for 1 hour. Transfer the formula into a container, cover with the lid, and gently shake to mix. When you are ready to use it, measure 1 teaspoon of the formula and place it on top of a hot charcoal block.

UNCROSSING INCENSE

Burn this incense to remove curses, jinxes, negative influences, or bad energies.

20 drops frankincense essential oil

20 drops myrrh essential oil

1 tablespoon clove powder

2 tablespoons galangal root powder

| 2 tablespoons | 3 tablespoons |
| hyssop powder | sandalwood powder |

Mix all of the liquid ingredients together in a mixing bowl. Mix all of the powder ingredients together in another mixing bowl. Slowly pour the dry ingredients into the liquid mixing bowl and stir. Transfer the formula to a baking pan and spread it evenly. Allow the formula to dry for 1 hour. Transfer the formula to a container, cover with the lid, and gently shake to mix. When you are ready to use it, measure 1 teaspoon of the formula and place it on top of a hot charcoal block.

PROTECTION INCENSE

Burn this incense to protect you from evil spirits and negative energies.

10 drops bergamot essential oil	1 tablespoon bay leaf powder
10 drops frankincense essential oil	1 tablespoon cinnamon
	2 tablespoons orange peel powder
10 drops lavender essential oil	1 tablespoon peppermint powder
2 tablespoons basil powder	

Mix all of the liquid ingredients together in a mixing bowl. Mix all of the powder ingredients together in another mixing bowl. Slowly pour the dry ingredients into the liquid mixing bowl and stir. Transfer the formula onto a baking pan a spread it evenly. Allow the formula to dry for 1 hour. Transfer the formula into a container, cover with a lid, and gently shake to mix. When you are ready to use it, measure 1 teaspoon of the formula and place it on top of a hot charcoal block.

DIVINATION AND PSYCHIC DEVELOPMENT INCENSE

Heighten your powers of divination with this powerful incense. Use it during or prior to performing psychic activities.

10 drops frankincense essential oil

10 drops lavender essential oil

10 drops myrrh essential oil

1 tablespoon anise powder

1 tablespoon bay leaf powder

3 tablespoons cinnamon powder

1 tablespoon nutmeg powder

1 tablespoon rose powder

Mix all of the liquid ingredients together in a mixing bowl. Mix all of the powder ingredients together in another mixing bowl. Slowly pour the dry ingredients into the liquid mixing bowl and stir. Transfer the formula onto a baking pan and spread it evenly. Allow the formula to dry for 1 hour. Transfer the formula into a container, cover with the lid, and gently shake to mix. When you are ready to use it, measure 1 teaspoon of the formula and place it on top of a hot charcoal block.

CHAPTER 7

POWDERS

In the rootwork tradition, powders are used in rituals to gain spiritual assistance from your ancestors, God, other deities, and spirit guides. To use powders, either blow or sprinkle the formulated ingredients onto or toward something. You can rub them on people or objects like charms or talismans to anoint them. Also, powders are a vital component of mojo bags. Sprinkle the powder inside the mojo bag for added strength.

In the past, some traditional rootwork ingredients used in making hoodoo powders—such as sulfur and talc— were quite harmful to the health and well-being of the humans, particularly children. Many generations ago, practitioners had limited scientific research to draw from regarding the safety of such ingredients for human use. Over time my family changed certain formulas to exclude the traditional ingredient as a safety precaution. For example, we substitute sulfur and talc with coconut flour, cornstarch powder, or rice flour, to name a few.

Hoodoo powders consist of a blend of herbs, flowers, roots, minerals, and carrier powders. During and after the powder-making process, continue to pray and ask for blessings for the purpose of the powder. You will need a mortar and pestle to grind any loose herbs to a fine powder unless all the ingredients that you buy are in powder form already.

Here is a list of multiple ways to use powders to help with your rituals and spells:

* Add it to bottle spells.
* Add it to floorwashes.
* Add it to incense formulas.
* Add it to honey jars.
* Dress ritual candles.
* Sprinkle on amulets.
* Sprinkle on charms.
* Sprinkle on clothing.
* Sprinkle on talismans.
* Sprinkle on business cards.
* Sprinkle on mojo bags.
* Sprinkle on objects, such as underneath your bedsheets, inside your pillowcase, inside your pockets, and in your hair conditioners and lotions.
* Sprinkle on petitions (see Chapter 12).
* Sprinkle on places, such as around the home or office.
* Sprinkle on vision boards.

MATERIALS

Here is a list of the essential supplies, essential oils, herbs and minerals, conjured oils, carrier oils, and carrier powders you will need to create the hoodoo powders in this chapter. Choose organic essential oils, herbs, minerals, and carrier oils whenever possible.

Essential supplies:

* Amber bottles or vials
* Baking pan
* Baking sheets
* Dropper
* Labels
* Lodestones (see page 141)
* Magnetic sand
* Mason jars: gallon (128 ounces), liter (33.8 ounces), quart (32 ounces), pint (16 ounces), half pint (8 ounces), and quarter pint (4 ounces)
* Measuring cups
* Measuring spoons
* Mesh strainer
* Minerals (organic)
* Mixing bowls
* Mortar and pestle
* Pen
* Pyrite
* Vitamin E oil (organic)
* Wooden spoons

Conjured oils types:

View Chapter 8: Oils for the formulated recipe blends.

* Love
  * Love-Drawing Oil
    (page 127)
  * New Love–Drawing
    Oil (page 133)
* Money
  * Fast-Money Oil
    (page 133)

* Success Oil
  (page 134)
* Uncrossing
  * Uncrossing Oil
    (page 129)
  * Uncrossing and
    Purification Oil
    (page 134)

Essential oil types:

* Basil
* Cinnamon
* Frankincense

* Lavender
* Patchouli

Herb and mineral types:

* Allspice powder
* Asafetida
* Basil
* Cinnamon powder
* Five finger grass
* Frankincense
* Garlic powder
* Hyssop
* Onion powder

* Orange peels
* Orris root powder
* Patchouli
* Peppermint leaves
* Rosebuds (pink,
  red, and white)
* Sandalwood powder
* Sea salt (black
  and white)

Carrier powders:

* Coconut flour
* Cornmeal
* Cornstarch
* Rice flour
* White flour

MAKING YOUR POWDERS

To make the powder, you will need to blend the herbs, flowers, minerals, and roots into a fine powder for ease of use. Then, mix all your dry ingredients together. Add the liquid ingredients and mix again. Dry the mixture completely, then add it to a mixing bowl and stir it to loosen it up. Transfer the formula to a storage container. Label your container with the name of the formula and the date. The expiration date of your powder will vary according to the ingredients you use. Some oils can remain fresh for up to a year while others must be discarded after a few months. As a rule, keep your powder for as long as the ingredient with the shortest shelf life allows.

LOVE-DRAWING POWDER

This powder is used to attract love to you.

1 tablespoon cinnamon powder

2 tablespoons sandalwood powder

1 teaspoon sweet basil

1 tablespoon cornstarch

10 drops frankincense essential oil

20 drops Love Oil

1 tablespoon red rosebud

Pour the cinnamon powder, sandalwood powder, and sweet basil into a mixing bowl. Mix all of the ingredients together well. Transfer the ingredients into a mortar and pestle to grind them into a fine powder, if needed. Add the cornstarch and mix it in thoroughly.

Return the formula to a mixing bowl. Add the frankincense essential oil and Love Oil, and mix. Prepare a baking pan with a baking sheet on top for easy cleanup. Transfer the mixture to the baking pan and spread it out evenly to dry. Once the formula is completely dry, add it to a mixing bowl and stir to loosen it up.

MONEY-DRAWING POWDER

This powder is used to draw money to you in the form of a new job, promotion, gambling win, gifts, etc.

1 teaspoon cinnamon powder

1 tablespoon five finger grass

2 tablespoons sandalwood powder

1 tablespoon cornstarch

15 drops Fast-Money Oil (page 133)

10 drops frankincense essential oil

10 drops patchouli essential oil

Pour the cinnamon powder, five finger grass, and sandalwood powder into a mixing bowl and mix them together well. Transfer the ingredients to a mortar and pestle to grind them into a fine powder, if needed. Add the cornstarch, and mix it in thoroughly.

Return the formula to a mixing bowl, then add the Money Oil blend, frankincense essential oil, and patchouli essential oil, and mix. Prepare a baking pan with a baking sheet on top. Transfer the mixture to the baking pan, spreading it out evenly to dry. Once the formula is completely dry, add it to a mixing bowl and stir to loosen it up.

PROSPERITY POWDER

Sprinkle this powder on your money altar, and it will give you abundance, wealth, and fast money. This powder will draw and attract prosperity to you.

1 teaspoon allspice powder

1 tablespoon cinnamon powder

1 teaspoon orange peels

1 teaspoon orris root powder

1 teaspoon patchouli

2 tablespoons sandalwood powder

2 tablespoons cornstarch

Pour everything but the cornstarch into a mixing bowl. Mix all of the ingredients together well. Transfer the ingredients to a mortar and pestle to grind them into a fine powder, if needed. Add the cornstarch and mix it in thoroughly.

BLESSINGS POWDER

This powder is great for bringing new blessings into your life, home, or workspace. It can also be used to heal, cleanse, and bring good luck.

2 tablespoons basil

1 teaspoon cinnamon powder

2 tablespoons peppermint leaves

2 tablespoons cornstarch powder

15 drops frankincense essential oil

15 drops lavender essential oil

Pour the basil, cinnamon powder, and peppermint leaves into a mixing bowl and mix them together well. Transfer the ingredients to a mortar and pestle to grind them into a fine powder, if needed. Add the cornstarch and mix it in thoroughly. Transfer the formula to a mixing bowl. Add the frankincense and lavender essential oils, and mix.

Prepare a baking pan with a baking sheet on top. Transfer the mixture to the baking pan, spreading it out evenly to dry. Once the formula is completely dry, add it to a mixing bowl and stir to loosen it up.

UNCROSSING POWDER

This powder is perfect for removing any jinxes, curses, negative energies, or evil spirits that have been placed on you or are surrounding you.

2 tablespoons hyssop

2 tablespoons sandalwood powder

1 teaspoon sea salt

2 tablespoons cornstarch

20 drops Uncrossing Oil (page 129)

Pour the hyssop, sandalwood powder, and sea salt into a mixing bowl and mix well. Transfer the ingredients to a mortar and pestle to grind into a fine powder, if needed. Add the cornstarch and mix it in thoroughly, then transfer the formula to a mixing bowl.

Add the uncrossing oil and mix. Prepare a baking pan with a baking sheet on top. Transfer the mixture onto the baking pan, spreading it out evenly to dry. Once the formula is completely dry, add it to a mixing bowl and stir to loosen it up.

STAY AWAY POWDER

Seven years ago, a new tenant in my office building bought the business next to my office. This person was very friendly but quickly became a nuisance. He regularly welcomed himself into my office to chat, offer massages, and ask odd and unnecessary questions. I planned to report him if this powder were to fail me. Luckily, after I sprinkled some Stay Away Powder in front of my office door, the unwanted visitor kept his distance and would just wave as he walked by my office. The power of prayer and a sprinkle of this powder kept him at bay.

2 tablespoons
asafetida powder

2 tablespoons black sea salt

1 teaspoon garlic powder

1 teaspoon onion powder

2 cups cornstarch

Pour the asafetida powder, black sea salt, garlic powder, and onion powder into a mixing bowl and mix together well. Transfer the ingredients to a mortar and pestle to grind them into a fine powder, if needed. Add the cornstarch and mix it in thoroughly. Transfer the formula to a storage container. Label your container with the name of the formula and the date.

CHAPTER 8

---✳---

OILS

---✳---

In the rootwork tradition, conjured oils are also known by other names, such as "anointing oils," "conditioned oils," and "hoodoo oils." The oils consist of a blend of various ingredients, including flowers, herbs, high-quality essential oils, roots, minerals, and carrier oils to create a powerful, goal-oriented infused formula. Amulets, charms, talismans, and personal matters are sometimes added depending on the purpose of the oil.

Oils play a key factor in ceremonial rituals. In early religious and spiritual traditions, like those of early Judaism, early Christianity, Zoroastrianism, early Mesopotamia, ancient Egypt, the Congo, and other African traditional religions like Vodun, oil was used to anoint the body for those being baptized, healing from illnesses, becoming initiated into a tradition or religion, and during marriage and other rituals. In rootwork tradition today, we continue to use oils for the same purposes as well as to give more power to achieving our intentions that we desire. Each essential oil has a unique fragrance that, when used, activates whatever emotions we're feeling at the time and any desires we wish to achieve. For example, if you want to manifest peace in your life, consider using chamomile or lavender oils to evoke a sense of relaxation in your life.

Crafting conjured oils takes time and commitment. Plan and choose your ingredients wisely; consider the shelf life of oils, and remember your intentions and how you will use the oil. As mentioned before, pray over your ingredients and materials, and ask for blessings for your purpose both prior to and after preparing your conjured oil.

Once you have completed making the oils, store them in a cool, dark area for at least 3 weeks. Alternatively, you may place them on a windowsill that receives a great amount of sun to allow the herbs to infuse into the oil for at least 3 weeks. Oils can last up to several months as long as no water gets introduced to the oil. When it comes in contact with water it goes rancid and becomes moldy.

There are multiple ways to use oils to help with your rituals and spells.

Here is a list of ways to use your oils:

* Add it to bottle spells.
* Add it to floorwashes.
* Add it to incense formulas.
* Add it to honey jars.
* Add it to spiritual baths.
* Anoint amulets.
* Anoint the body.
* Anoint charms.
* Anoint talismans.
* Anoint business cards.
* Anoint clothing.
* Anoint mojo bags.
* Anoint petitions.
* Anoint places, such as the home or office.
* Anoint vision boards.
* Dress ritual candles.
* Use it as perfume.

MATERIALS

Choose organic essential oils, herbs, and minerals whenever possible. For the body oils, it is also best to use organic carrier oils that work great with your skin type. Adding vitamin E oil as an extra ingredient may increase the shelf life of your body oil and provide an extra benefit for your skin. Feel free to alter the formulas to best suit you, keeping your health and well-being first in mind. Consider what works best for your skin when choosing a carrier oil.

Here is a list of the essential supplies, essential oils, herbs and minerals, and carrier oils you will need to create the conjured oils in this chapter. The carrier oils are grouped for different skin types.

Essential supplies

* Amber vials or bottles
* Crystals and stones
  * Clear quartz
  * Lodestone
  * Magnetic sand
  * Rose quartz
  * Pyrite
* Dropper
* Labels
* Mason jars: gallon (128 oz.), liter (33.8 oz.), quart (32 oz.), pint (16 oz.), half pint (8 oz.), and quarter pint (4 oz.)
* Measuring cups
* Measuring spoons
* Mesh strainer
* Mixing bowls
* Mortar and pestle
* Pen
* Vitamin E oil (organic)
* Wooden spoons

Essential oil types

* Basil
* Bergamot
* Cedarwood
* Cinnamon
* Clover
* Frankincense
* Hyssop
* Jasmine
* Lavender
* Lemon
* Myrrh
* Nutmeg
* Patchouli
* Peppermint

* Rose
* Rosemary
* Sage

* Sandalwood
* Thyme

Herb and mineral types

* Anise star pods
* Basil
* Bay leaves
* Cinnamon powder
* Cinnamon sticks
* Five finger grass
* Galangal root
* High John the Conquer root
* Hyssop
* Lavender buds

* Lemon verbena
* Lemongrass
* Magnetic sand
* Myrrh powder
* Peppermint
* Rosebuds (pink, red, and white)
* Rosemary
* Sandalwood powder
* Sea salt
* Vetiver root leaves

Carrier oil types

Normal skin

* Apricot kernel oil
* Argan oil
* Coconut oil
* Grapeseed oil
* Sunflower seed oil

Dry skin

* Avocado oil
* Jojoba oil
* Olive oil
* Rosehip oil
* Sweet almond oil
* Sunflower seed oil

Oily skin

* Grapeseed oil
* Jojoba oil
* Sweet almond oil

Acne-prone skin

* Grapeseed oil
* Hemp seed oil
* Jojoba oil
* Rosehip oil

Combination skin

* Jojoba oil

Sensitive skin

* Apricot oil
* Jojoba oil
* Sesame seed oil
* Sweet almond oil

CONJURED BODY OILS

Body oils anoint your body with the specific properties that correlate to your desires and goals. They can be used on your entire body similar to applying a lotion or moisturizer, or they can be used only on the forehead, pressure points, or behind the ears or collarbones. Depending on the type of herbs, essential oils, and carrier oils used, it would be best to anoint yourself on the forehead, wrists, collarbones, or behind the ears for starters. Use one after taking a spiritual bath to maximize your goals and turn your intentions into reality. These oils may also be used to anoint objects, dress candles, and so forth.

The following formulas call for specific amounts of essential oils. Use only high-quality essential oils that you are able to use topically. Add vitamin E oil to preserve the shelf life.

Vitamin E oil is an antioxidant and slows the oil from oxidizing and going rancid. It also has the symbolic meaning of extending life or specific intent of a spell due to the natural properties it has, representing longevity.

If you are not familiar with diluting essential oils in carrier oils, please consult with an aromatherapist. Remember, to make a 2 percent dilution, add 10 to 12 drops of essential oil to each ounce of carrier oil. If you are crafting your own conjured oils, make sure you plan out your measurements before mixing the oils altogether.

SKIN PATCH TEST

As a safety rule, do a skin patch test with any essential oil or carrier oil that is new to you to make sure it will not give you a bad reaction.

To do a skin patch test, mix 1 to 2 drops of each essential oil required in the formula with 2 tablespoons of your chosen carrier oil. Apply the mixture to your inner elbow. Allow 48 hours to check for any allergic reactions and sensitivities, such as inflammation, signs of irritation, itchiness, or redness at the site. Should you have any type of reaction within the 48 hours, immediately wash the area with your normal body soap and apply moisturizer. Contact your health-care provider immediately for health emergencies and speak to your physician for an allergy test.

These oils may also be used for all other purposes that fit your intentions that requires you to anoint objects, dressing candles, and so forth.

Directions

1. Pour the carrier oil and the vitamin E oil into a mixing bowl.

2. Add the essential oils to the bowl. Mix all of the ingredients together well. Transfer the formula to your chosen container with a lid.

3. Transfer a small amount of the formula into glass vials for travel use.

4. Label the containers with the name, formula ingredients, and date to keep track of shelf life.

5. Store in a cool, dark area. Use a generous amount as needed.

SUCCESS AND BUSINESS ENDEAVORS OIL

In business, career, and wealth, this oil will give you plenty of fortune and affluence.

1 cup jojoba carrier oil

½ cup vitamin E oil

20 drops bergamot essential oil

15 drops cinnamon essential oil

10 drops peppermint essential oil

GOOD LUCK AND FORTUNE OIL

This oil will make you very lucky and triumphant in an unpredictable area.

1 cup jojoba carrier oil

½ cup vitamin E oil

20 drops cinnamon essential oil

10 drops lemon essential oil

15 drops patchouli essential oil

GAME OF CHANCE OIL

Use this oil to win big in lottery, gambling, or other games of chance.

1 cup jojoba carrier oil

½ cup vitamin E oil

15 drops basil essential oil

20 drops cedarwood essential oil

10 drops clover essential oil

MONEY-DRAWING OIL

This oil will specifically magnetize money to you in spades.

1 cup jojoba carrier oil

½ cup vitamin E oil

20 drops cinnamon essential oil

15 drops nutmeg essential oil

10 drops peppermint essential oil

ATTRACTING PROSPERITY OIL

Riches, profits, and abundance will come your way when you use this oil.

1 cup jojoba carrier oil

½ cup vitamin E oil

15 drops cinnamon essential oil

10 drops nutmeg essential oil

20 drops sandalwood essential oil

LOVE-DRAWING OIL

Use this oil to attract all forms of love into your life.

1 cup jojoba carrier oil

½ cup vitamin E oil

10 drops cinnamon essential oil

20 drops patchouli essential oil

15 drops rose essential oil

COME TO ME NOW OIL

This oil attracts love and affection to you. Use it if you want a specific person to come to you immediately.

1 cup jojoba carrier oil

½ cup vitamin E oil

20 drops cinnamon essential oil

10 drops nutmeg essential oil

15 drops rose essential oil

ATTRACT AND DESIRE OIL

This oil serves as a natural magnet. It can be used to magnetically attract love, success, or money to you.

1 cup jojoba carrier oil

½ cup vitamin E oil

10 drops cinnamon essential oil

20 drops frankincense essential oil

15 drops rose essential oil

APHRODISIAC SEDUCTION OIL

This oil can help enhance your sensual and sexual energy.

1 cup jojoba carrier oil

½ cup vitamin E oil

10 drops jasmine essential oil

20 drops rose essential oil

15 drops sandalwood essential oil

HOLY OIL

This oil is great for ritual ceremonies. It can be used to bless objects, people, and places.

1 cup jojoba carrier oil

½ cup vitamin E oil

20 drops hyssop essential oil

20 drops frankincense essential oil

UNCROSSING OIL

Use this oil if any jinxes, hexes, or curses have been placed on you. It'll help neutralize your energy.

1 cup jojoba carrier oil

½ cup vitamin E oil

15 drops frankincense essential oil

20 drops hyssop essential oil

10 drops myrrh essential oil

PROTECTION OIL

Use this oil to protect yourself from any negative spirits or evils.

1 cup jojoba carrier oil

½ cup vitamin E oil

10 drops basil essential oil

10 drops bergamot essential oil

20 drops frankincense essential oil

20 drops lavender essential oil

PSYCHIC PROTECTION OIL

This oil will help ward off any curses, spells, or attacks from psychics.

1 cup jojoba carrier oil

½ cup vitamin E oil

20 drops cedarwood essential oil

20 drops hyssop essential oil

SACRED HEALING OIL

This oil helps promote a healthy lifestyle. Use it if you are recovering from injury or illness.

1 cup jojoba carrier oil

½ cup vitamin E oil

10 drops rosemary essential oil

20 drops sage essential oil

15 drops thyme essential oil

FERTILITY OIL

Use this oil to boost your chances to conceive. It can also be used to clear any blockages that may be preventing fertility or creation.

1 cup jojoba carrier oil

½ cup vitamin E oil

20 drops hyssop essential oil

20 drops rose essential oil

DIVINATION AND PSYCHIC DEVELOPMENT OIL

This oil can help increase your psychic energies and awareness and improve your overall psychic work.

1 cup jojoba carrier oil

½ cup vitamin E oil

| 20 drops cinnamon essential oil | 15 drops lavender essential oil |
| 20 drops frankincense essential oil | 15 drops myrrh essential oil |

CONJURED OILS WITH DRIED HERBS

The following formulas consist of a blend of organic herbs and minerals infused with organic carrier oils for all-purpose use in rituals and spells. Add vitamin E oil to preserve the shelf life. Each formula creates a generous amount so you can share with others.

Directions

1. Mix the herbs, spices, if using, and magnetic sand together in a mixing bowl. Transfer the mixture to a 16-ounce jar.

2. Add the High John the Conqueror root and the healing stone(s) to the jar.

3. Slowly pour the liquid ingredients to cover the herbs inside the jar. If the herbs surface to the top, refill the jar with olive oil to keep them covered. Allow a minimum of 3 inches of space between the formula and lid to allow the herbs to expand in the mixture.

4. Cover the jar with the lid and tighten. Gently shake the jar a few times to mix the formula. Label the container with the name, date, and formula ingredients.

5. Store the jar in a cool, dark area for three weeks. Every week, check and observe the formula to make sure that the oils and herbs have not separated. If they have, shake the container a few times to mix. Alternatively, you may place the jar on a windowsill with full sun exposure for three weeks. Again, observe the formula and shake the container to mix if the contents have separated.

6. After three weeks, strain the herbs out of the oil using a mesh strainer. Transfer the remaining infused oil to a clean jar or vials. Label your containers with the name, date, and formula ingredients.

7. The conjured oil with dried herbs is now ready to use. Store it in a cool, dark area when not in use to preserve the oil's shelf life.

VAN-VAN OIL

Use this oil to attract positive, influential people into your life, remove any negative energies that you may experience, and increase your luck with money and love.

¼ cup lemongrass

¼ cup lemon verbena

¼ cup vetiver root leaves

1 to 3 tablespoons magnetic sand

1 High John the Conqueror root

1 lodestone

2 cups olive carrier oil

½ cup vitamin E oil

FAST-MONEY OIL

Use this oil to attract quick luck with money and finances, gambling, or the lottery.

¼ cup cinnamon powder

¼ cup bay leaves

1 to 3 tablespoons magnetic sand

¼ cup peppermint leaves

1 High John the Conqueror root

1 lodestone

1 pyrite

2 cups olive carrier oil

½ cup vitamin E oil

NEW LOVE-DRAWING OIL

Similar to the Love-Drawing Oil (see page 127), this oil specifically attracts new love to you.

¼ cup cinnamon powder

¼ cup lavender buds

1 to 3 tablespoons magnetic sand

¼ cup peppermint leaves

¼ cup rosebuds

1 High John the Conqueror root

1 lodestone

1 rose quartz

2 cups olive carrier oil

½ cup vitamin E oil

JUSTICE AND LEGAL OIL

Use this oil to level the playing fields in court or legal cases. It can also be used to seek justice when you have been wronged or help you win in court against any unjust charges that have been brought against you.

- ¼ cup cinnamon powder
- ¼ cup galangal root
- 1 to 3 tablespoons magnetic sand
- ¼ cup star anise pods
- 1 High John the Conqueror root
- 1 lodestone
- 1 pyrite
- 2 cups olive carrier oil
- ½ cup vitamin E oil

SUCCESS OIL

Use this oil if you are seeking success in your life.

- ¼ cup cinnamon powder
- ¼ cup five finger grass
- 1 to 3 tablespoons magnetic sand
- ¼ cup sandalwood oil or powder
- 1 High John the Conqueror root
- 1 lodestone
- 2 cups olive carrier oil
- ½ cup vitamin E oil

UNCROSSING AND PURIFICATION OIL

Use this oil to drive away evil and banish negative spirits and energies from your life. It can also be used to cleanse your energy and return it to a balanced state.

- ¼ cup hyssop
- ¼ cup myrrh oil or powder
- ¼ cup sandalwood oil or powder
- 1 teaspoon sea salt
- 1 clear quartz
- 2 cups olive carrier oil
- ½ cup vitamin E oil

CHAPTER 9

CRYSTALS AND STONES

Crystals and stones are a gift from nature. Packed with miraculous properties, they naturally retain and magnify energies like nothing else. They're powerful, activated with the energies of the earth and the specific origin from which they come.

Crystals and stones work wonders for those who choose to form a partnership with them. You may use them alone for healing purposes, combine them with other crystals for multiple purposes, or combine them with other spiritual tools for your rituals and spells. Ultimately, a crystal or stone will enhance your intentions based on its specific properties.

In the rootwork tradition, crystals and stones are mainly used as amulets or ingredients for conjure waters, mojo bags, and spiritual baths. Another common use is for altar placement, where they represent the ancestors and the earth element. The main purpose for using crystals and stones in hoodoo is to provide protection by dispelling negativity and enhancing energetic properties by attracting your intentions toward you. The most common crystals and stones that my ancestors used were copper, gold, jade, lodestone, pyrite, silver, turquoise, and quartz. I learned to use these types as a child and slowly grew my collection to include the most common crystals and stones used in rootwork tradition today.

You'll find a vast number of crystals and stones locally in stores and online. Be sure to select only natural quality crystals and stones. In addition, you may find a direct seller or visit a gem show to find the perfect match for you. Gem shows are usually seasonal and last for a few days only. I personally love going to gem shows because you get to meet direct sellers who know the source from which they purchased the crystals and stones; plus, the diversity is breathtaking! You should definitely add a gem show to your bucket list at least once in your lifetime.

Another unforgettable alternative at the top of my list is visiting a gemstone mine that is open to the public. You're able to explore and experience extracting nature's gifts yourself for a fee. The crystals and stones found in their shops are directly from the mine that you're visiting.

A wide variety of crystals and stones can be found in the United States. Thirteen states have mines that are open to the public. I suggest researching the mines you would like to visit here or anywhere in the world and see which gemstones are available. Remember to always give your thanks and praises for nature's gifts, especially when you have the opportunity of a lifetime to extract your own crystals and stones.

Here are the states with mines open to the public:

* Arizona
* Arkansas
* California
* Colorado
* Idaho
* Louisiana
* Maine
* Montana
* Nevada
* North Carolina
* Oregon
* Tennessee
* Utah

The following crystals and stones can be found in US mines:

* Agate
* Beryl
* Diamond
* Garnet
* Jade
* Jasper
* Opal
* Peridot
* Quartz
* Sapphire
* Topaz
* Tourmaline
* Turquoise

The crystals and stones that I currently use hold a special place in my heart. Before my beloved grandmother Mary Ree passed four years ago, she enjoyed having crystal healing sessions. I visited her—both at home and in the hospital whenever she was placed in the ICU—to provide energetic healing with the assistance of specific crystals. Most of the time, I used amethyst or quartz to keep energies clear, especially when health-care personnel were in and out of her hospital room throughout the day. Whenever my grandma was in need of chakra healing, I used gems that represent each main chakra center. Keeping your chakras aligned is essential to your emotional, physical, and spiritual well-being. My grandma always enjoyed these therapeutic sessions and often held the amethyst or citrine crystals in her hand before physical therapy.

Besides using crystals and stones with my beloved grandma, I also used them during in-person and distance crystal-healing sessions for clients, animals, friends, and family. They are simple to use as spiritual healing tools, once you develop a partnership with them. It may take some time, but the more you practice with nature's gifts, the more you'll sense and develop a lasting relationship with them.

In addition to healing tools, crystals and stones are also great to use for jewelry. My Filipino grandmother Ederlinda, who I call Nanay (means mom in Tagalog), harnesses crystals and stones for their positive and beautiful energetic properties as jewelry pieces. She has gifted me with lovely bracelets, rings, and sets that I wear during ceremonial rituals and special occasions, and place on my altars for enhancing my goals and intentions. This family tradition of gifting family members crystals and stones led me to create my own jewelry line and divination pieces that I offer as gifts and products for my clients.

Cherish every crystal and stone you come across, especially if you sense a strong attraction to them. These gifts of nature may lead you to help not only yourself but also be of service to others.

TOP COMMON CRYSTALS AND STONES

Amazonite: A milky green stone, excellent for soothing the mind and body (it is mainly used for the physical and spiritual well-being of females). Amazonite enhances the nervous system and clears thoughts. Emitting a green hue, amazonite is great for inducing good fortune upon yourself or others.

Amethyst: The properties of this violet crystal are broad and positive. Amethysts avert negativity, tension, and spiritual harm from the holder. As much as it averts, it brings; amethysts induce enthused transformation, assisting those who seek its help to avoid addictive drinking, drug abuse, smoking, and gambling. Oriented with the Crown Chakra, amethysts are known to soothe anxiety in both the quiescent and waken mind.

Aquamarine: The crystal representing the Throat Chakra influences positivity in spoken word, interviews, and train of thought. Aquamarine is a soft blue crystal that enhances the holder's vocal power. In addition, aquamarine is a crystal that differentiates lie from truth, encouraging the speaker to tell the truth in a calm manner.

Azurite: Like an ocean, azurite is a mix of deep blues and vibrant greens. Azurites support spiritual awakening, meditation, and controlling one's fears. Physically, azurite can heal tendons and muscle pain. It is mostly used for the back.

Carnelian: Another form of agate but in shades of orange. Carnelian's connected to the Sacral Chakra, using that chakra to enhance grounding, fertility, and a dome of safe thoughts. This orange stone improves concentration and communication. Along with improving expression of speech, carnelian is a great crystal that blooms career and social success.

Citrine: Citrine has evolved into two types: madeira citrine and golden citrine. Madeira citrine consists of orange-brown hues, while golden citrine has yellow-gold shades. Although different in color, their properties are identical. Citrines represent the Solar Plexus Chakra. Citrine manifests creativity, endurance, prosperity, confidence, and success. Using the

Naval Chakra, citrine improves self-esteem and helps with food disorders such as anorexia, bulimia, and obesity.

Diamond: A crystal valuable to clairvoyants, diamonds have the opacity of a prism. Diamonds manifest purity, strength, power, and protection from malevolent omens. Diamonds are commonly known as amplifiers, strengthening anything from which the holder is surrounded by. If the holder is surrounded by good energy, diamonds will strengthen the good energy; however, it will do the same for negative aspects if the holder experiences negative emotions.

Jade: Mainly known for its beautiful hues of green, jade is also found in black, blue, brown, orange, purple, and white. Jade radiates with energies of good fortune and luck. This amazing crystal also brings emotional and physical healing to the holder, plus amplifies the intentions of good health. Using this crystal will also bring a calming and just state of mind.

Kyanite: This ridged stone has two forms: black kyanite and blue kyanite. With the appearance of a skyscraper, it is useful for psychic sight. Kyanite influences serene meditation, channeling lucid and vivid dreams and thoughts to reality. Kyanite is also used to open a clear visualization into one's past lives.

Lodestone: A unique metallic stone that is naturally magnetic, lodestone is gifted with the power of attraction. This stone is one of a kind and a must-have for all who desire balance, protection, and success. Lodestone's potent energies are a great source for energy healing, intuitive development, and grounding.

Pyrite: With its gold-like appearance, pyrite is known as fool's gold. Pyrite is believed to channel success, creativity, spiritual growth, and wealth. Pyrite, or iron pyrite, is an element that heals iron deficiency and anemia.

Quartz: Quartz has multiple forms, each with similar yet specific properties: blue quartz soothes emotional strain; rock crystal quartz influences exuberant energy; rose quartz symbolizes compassion, peace, and love; rutilated quartz increases willpower and self-indulgence; smoky quartz eliminates negative energy while attracting positive energy; snow quartz associates with tranquility, meditative energy, and reflection.

Tiger's-eye: A silky stone of red, gold, bronze, and black, tiger's-eye is an iridescent element. Associated with the Root Chakra, tiger's-eye helps with aching bones, irritable bowel syndrome, and stress. Tiger's-eye represents self-confidence, harmony, protection from vice and the emotions of enemies, and wisdom. Tiger's-eye stabilizes one's spiritual focus as well.

Topaz: Topaz can meld into blue and yellow types: blue topaz influences growth, concentration, guidance, and lucidity; yellow topaz associates itself with the Solar Plexus Chakra, helping with sleep, stress, willpower, dreams and other realms, and tranquility of mind and body.

Tourmaline: This stone comes in two varieties, green and watermelon; however, both serve similar purposes. Tourmaline balances the forces in the body, also known as solar and lunar, yin and yang, masculine and feminine. Tourmaline dissolves blood clots and treats high and low blood pressure.

CRYSTALS AND STONES PREPARATION AND PURIFICATION

Prepare your crystals and stones accordingly, prior to using them. This is essential, making sure it is connected to your body, mind, and soul. It also assures it cannot be used by anyone else, and that its results will always serve you and who you serve. Preparing your gem includes purifying and cleansing your gem. Doing this will link its energy to yours.

CLEANSING RITUAL

Hold the gem under lustrous water for 5 to 10 minutes to start the cleansing process. You may use rainwater or holy water (see Chapters 4 and 5). Then, place the gem on a clean plate made of natural resources and place the plate under the full moon overnight. Alternatively, you may place it in full sun exposure for a short period of time or however long intuitively feels right to you. Once the gem is done soaking in the light, give thanks for the cleansing process removing any negative and unwanted energies.

PURIFICATION RITUAL

The purification follows a similar process. Find a bowl made of any natural resource rather than plastic or metal. Place your gem in the bowl along with water and a pinch of salt. Leave your gem in the bowl for a few hours while exerting your intention into your gem. Manifesting your energy and intention into your gem will prepare it for its spiritual duties–your intention is the gem's goal.

As you fill your gem with your intention, make sure to be near it or place your hands above or around the bowl. You are nurturing the gem until it gets used to the feel of your energy. Once you are done, dry the gem with a clean cloth. Place it inside a pouch or wrap it in a beautiful cotton or bamboo cloth for protection. Keep the gem with you at all times for at least a week to align your energies together before using it.

Once you complete this process, you'll start to sense the energies of the gem with a variety of sensations. Place the gem in your hand and take notes regarding the type of sensation you feel as you develop a partnership with the gem. Some feel warmth, such as a temperature change from cold to hot, or vice versa. Some feel a tingling or a throbbing sensation. Everyone experiences it differently.

ALTERNATIVE USES FOR CRYSTALS AND STONES

Crystals and stones can be used for purposes other than healing or setting rituals or spells. Many people wear them as jewelry or hang them as decorative pieces. Here are several other uses for crystals and stones:

Altar: Add to table or sacred spaces.

Bed and pillow: Place under pillows for protection. Amethyst is wonderful for keeping nightmares away, especially for children.

Candles: Add extra energy to your candle magick rituals and spells.

Conjure waters and floorwashes: Add inside the bottles to enhance the formula with the properties of the gem. Quartz is a healing gem to add to blessed water.

Divination tools: Use as divination tools, such as a pendulum or to assist with card readings.

Home: Add larger clusters to the decor of your home. Large amethyst clusters are great for positive and healing energies.

Car: Place inside your car for safe travels.

Clothing: Add to daily attire or ceremonial clothing.

Jewelry: Add to earrings, bracelets, necklaces, waist beads, etc.

Mojo bags: Add specific gems to mojo bags to enhance powers.

Spiritual baths: Add specific gems that fit the intentions of the spiritual bath formula for extra power.

TOP CRYSTALS AND STONES FOR ASTROLOGICAL SIGNS

Here is a list of crystals and stones associated with each astrological sign.

Aries (March 21 to April 19)

- Amethyst
- Black onyx
- Garnet
- Topaz
- Diamond

Taurus (April 20 to May 20)

- Agate
- Citrine
- Emerald
- Jade
- Sapphire

Gemini (May 21 to June 20)

- Agate
- Aquamarine
- Emerald
- Tiger's-eye
- Topaz

Cancer (June 21 to July 22)

- Carnelian
- Citrine
- Emerald
- Rose quartz
- Ruby
- Selenite

Leo (July 23 to August 22)

- Black tourmaline
- Diamond
- Garnet
- Rose quartz
- Ruby

Virgo (August 23 to September 22)

- Amethyst
- Aventurine
- Carnelian
- Jasper
- Sapphire

Libra (September 23 to October 22)

- Aquamarine
- Blue tiger's-eye
- Jade
- Sapphire
- Turquoise

Scorpio (October 23 to November 21)

- Black tourmaline
- Carnelian
- Jasper
- Rose quartz
- Topaz

Sagittarius (November 22 to December 21)

- Citrine
- Jasper
- Lapis lazuli
- Topaz
- Turquoise

Capricorn (December 22 to January 19)

- Azurite
- Emerald
- Garnet
- Red tiger's-eye
- Ruby

Aquarius (January 20 to February 18)

- Amethyst
- Garnet
- Jade
- Rose quartz
- Sapphire

Pisces (February 19 to March 20)

- Amethyst
- Aquamarine
- Carnelian
- Clear quartz
- Lapis lazuli

CRYSTALS AND STONES FOR CHAKRA HEALING

To use crystals and stones for chakra healing, find a comfortable position. Ideally, it is best to lie in a supine position (on your back) or comfortably in a seated position if you are not able to be in a supine position. Place your hand directly over each chakra center or 3 to 12 inches away. It is best to start with the first chakra, the root chakra. It is the base that grounds you into the Earth and into your being. Hold your hand in that position, taking mental notes of any emotional or even physical sensations. If you feel a sensation, hold a clear quartz (perfect gem for all chakras) or the proper gem in your hand to activate that feeling. Once you feel a connection, you are ready to place it in the proper chakra position as described below.

If you do not feel a sensation while your hands are over a chakra center, move on to the next. Once you have the gem in the proper position, allow yourself to relax and the energy to flow until you intuitively feel it is ready to move on. With practice, you will become more aware and develop your own technique. Remember, you may not feel a sensation right away, so have patience with yourself as you embark on this simple technique for crystal healing.

THE CROWN CHAKRA

Use: Healing for Enlightenment and Spiritual Connection

Method: Gently place the gem on top of your head or hold it a few inches away from the top of your head. Allow the energy of the gem to intertwine with your own. If you sense that the energy healing is complete, move on to the next or conclude the process by giving thanks.

Use one of these gems: Amethyst, Clear quartz, or Selenite

THE THIRD EYE CHAKRA

Use: Healing for Intuitive Development and Spiritual Awakening

Use one of these gems: Gently place the gem between the eyes or hold it a few inches above the center between the eyes.

Use one of these gems: Amethyst, Kyanite, or Lapis lazuli

THE THROAT CHAKRA

Use: Healing for Authentic Communication and Expression

Use one of these gems: Gently place the gem on the center of your throat or hold it a few inches above the center of your throat.

Use one of these gems: Aquamarine, Sapphire, or Turquoise

THE HEART CHAKRA

Use: Healing for Compassion and Unconditional Love

Use one of these gems: Gently place the gem on the center of your chest or hold it a few inches above the center of your chest.

Use one of these gems: Agate, Jade, or Rose quartz

THE SOLAR PLEXUS CHAKRA

Use: Healing for Strength and Transformational Development

Use one of these gems: Gently place the gem 3 inches above your navel or hold it a few inches above the 3 inches from your navel.

Use one of these gems: Amber, Citrine, or Topaz

THE SACRAL CHAKRA

Use: Healing for Creativity and Emotional Intelligence

Use one of these gems: Gently place the gem on the genital area or hold it a few inches above the genital area.

Use one of these gems: Amber, Carnelian, or Tiger's-eye

THE ROOT CHAKRA

Use: Healing for Grounding and Life Force Energy

Use one of these gems: Gently place the gem at the base of your spine/tailbone while lying on your stomach or hold it a few inches above the base of your spine/tailbone.

Use one of these gems: Black tourmaline, Red jasper, or Tiger's-eye

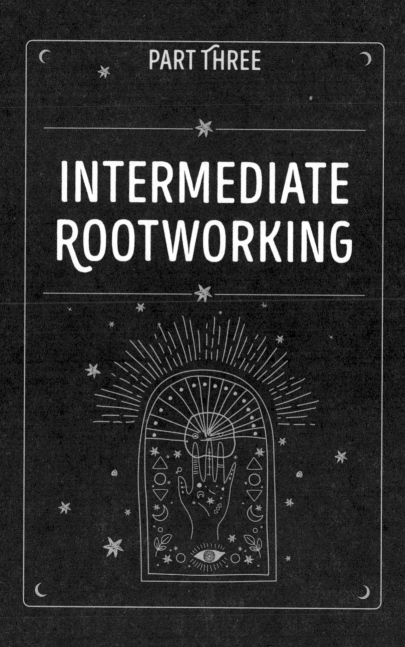

PART THREE

INTERMEDIATE ROOTWORKING

CHAPTER 10

AMULETS, CHARMS, TALISMANS

AMULETS

In the rootwork tradition, an amulet is usually a tiny object that attracts something toward the wearer and dispels and protects the wearer from unwanted influences. The wearer can be a person, place, or thing. Similar to charms and talismans, amulets are usually made from natural materials like plants and stones, bones, and other preserved animal parts. Amulets usually find their way to you, or you'll experience a magnetic pull to partner up with a protection object.

Sometimes you'll find that people will gift you with protection medals in the form of a coin, jewelry, or accessory to add to your vehicle or home. Many years ago, for example, a childhood friend James gifted me an Archangel Michael (also known as St. Michael) metal pin for the car for protection and safe travels while on the road. I also remember a time when my best friend Monika took a rosary from one of my vehicles and placed it in our rental vehicle for protection before we took a small road trip to another state.

Another popular amulet is an ankh necklace. The ankh represents the divine feminine and masculine energies, plus everlasting life. It may also protect from disease and sickness. Begin to take notice of all the amulets that are currently surrounding you.

The most common amulets you'll find are:

Alligator foot: for drawing money and good luck in gambling

Catclaw: for drawing power and luck

Crab powder: for reversing spells against you or someone else

Crossbone: for absorbing negative and unwanted energies

Rabbit foot: for fertility and good luck

Raccoon genitalia bone: for attracting new love

Wishbone: for good luck and wishes

CHARMS

A charm is similar to an amulet but is usually worn on the body in secret, visible only to the wearer. The purpose of individual charms is to attract good luck or any intentions you may desire. Charms can range in size and material. Charm items include but are not limited to crystals, herbs, roots, metals, and stones.

In the rootwork tradition, charms can consist of conjured bags, gris-gris bags, medicine bags, or mojo bags. This form of magick is prepared at an altar with consecrated items that will assist you with attracting an intention toward you or dispel something unwanted away from you. They are placed in a small flannel or drawstring bag with an odd number of items handpicked by you or a rootworker. The number of items may range from one through thirteen. Item types can include bones, crystals, herbs, minerals, roots, stones, oils, and symbols that associate with the purpose of the charm bag. You may also add in personal matters, such as hair, nails, or pieces of cloth used by you or another individual to imbue the bag with that fixed energy.

Once you finish making your charm bag, place it away from the public eye. Preferably, the bag can be placed around your neck or under your shirt, pinned inside your clothing, or placed in a pocket. Whenever you feel the need to recharge your charm bag, anoint it with a specific oil that was used throughout the making of your bag or in conjunction to your intentions and purposes. As an example, my charm bag is packed with herbs and items for good luck and money drawing. I use a money oil to anoint my charm bag, recharging the energy of the bag either on a daily or weekly basis.

TALISMANS

A talisman is a very specific item of power made with an inscription created during a specific astrological time that aligns the planets or stars with the wearer's intention. For a true talisman, the astrological aspect is vital because it means that particular talisman was created at the right time and with the proper materials for durability and longevity.

Rootworkers prepare talismans or wear them themselves for magickal or religious protection. The talisman object may attract a specific purpose or protect from unwanted influences. A talisman is usually in the form of:

* clothing
* a portable object such as a coin or jewelry pendant

* parchment paper with a bible verse, a magickal symbol, or sigil drawn or printed on it

Regardless of what the talisman is, the primary purpose is to attract positive energies to you indefinitely.

To create a talisman, first choose the object that you bear a connection to. It can be made from any material. Then, determine the purpose of your talisman. Are you using it to attract love or increase financial gain? Will it be used to protect you? Once you have done this, it's time to charge your talisman. Spend time pouring positive intentions and energies into the object. You can choose a prayer or a mantra to speak into the base of your talisman.

Use your talisman in moments of happiness or excitement and place it away from you when you're feeling sad so that your talisman doesn't absorb any negative energies. After each use, remember to charge it so that it maintains its effectiveness. To recharge your talisman, repeat positive intentions into it like you did when first creating it. Or, similar to recharging your charm bag, you can anoint your talisman with an oil that matches your intentions.

CHAPTER 11

✳

BIBLE AND PRAYERS

✳

The Bible is central to rituals and spells in the rootwork tradition. You'll be surprised at what you can find in the Good Book that can assist you with all types of matters. Don't worry, even if you choose not to use the Bible in your personal practice, you can still carry out meaningful rootwork without it. This chapter is more for those who have the desire to incorporate the Bible or who are curious to learn more.

There are specific prayers in the Bible, such as Glory Be, Hail Mary, and The Lord's Prayer, that are often used in conjunction with spells. There are also verses in the Bible that help with manifesting intentions into reality. Psalms is one of the most popular books in the Bible to work with. As mentioned in other chapters, Psalm 23 is my grandma's favorite verse. I use this verse for all matters, especially for money rituals and spells. Here's a select list of psalms and what area in your life it can bolster.

* **Psalm 1** will assist with bringing and maintaining peace inside the home.

* **Psalm 3** will assist with spiritual strength for stressful situations.

* **Psalm 4** will assist with matters of luck, including increasing your chances of winning in games, contests, and lotteries.

* **Psalm 5** will assist with matters of law and order, increasing your chances of gaining favor with a judge.

* **Psalm 10** will assist with dispelling negative energies and spirits.

* **Psalm 16** will assist with resolving problems with an enemy.

* **Psalm 20** will assist with a positive verdict for matters of law.

* **Psalm 23** will assist with illness.

* **Psalm 26** will assist with an early release date for an incarcerated individual.

* **Psalm 28** will assist with gaining financial success if your intentions and prayers are directed toward this matter. Alternatively, this psalm will also assist with matters of reconciliation.

- **Psalm 32** will assist with God's grace.
- **Psalm 35** will assist with receiving financial help. Also, similar to Psalm 5, this psalm will also assist with matters of law, especially if your case is against an unjust individual.
- **Psalm 36** will assist with protection from gossip.
- **Psalm 41** will assist with attracting material needs toward you.
- **Psalm 45** will assist with receiving financial help from a lover. Also, this psalm will assist with marriage reconciliation.
- **Psalm 47** will assist with keeping a positive and respected reputation.
- **Psalm 50** will assist with the protection of any wrongdoing planned against you.
- **Psalm 57** will assist with good luck in general.
- **Psalm 61** will assist with blessing your home and bringing in good luck.
- **Psalm 62** will assist with blessings.
- **Psalm 63** will assist with overcoming loss and problems from business deals gone bad.
- **Psalm 65** will assist with the success of your intentions into reality.
- **Psalm 66** will assist with undoing evil spirit possession.
- **Psalm 67** will assist with financial abundance and blessings.

- ✳ **Psalm 69** will assist with releasing bad habits.
- ✳ **Psalm 70** will assist with overcoming an enemy or competitor.
- ✳ **Psalm 72** will assist with attracting money toward you.
- ✳ **Psalm 73** will assist with winning the lottery.
- ✳ **Psalm 87** will assist with making the right choices.
- ✳ **Psalm 98** will assist with peace and harmony between families.
- ✳ **Psalm 99** will assist with spiritual support that is needed.
- ✳ **Psalm 109** will assist with protecting you from an enemy.
- ✳ **Psalm 122** will assist with safe travels.
- ✳ **Psalm 133** will assist with friendships and gaining more meaningful relationships.
- ✳ **Psalm 137** will assist with releasing negative and unwanted feelings.

The Songs of Solomon is another favorite book for matters of love, especially for returning a lover or attracting a new love toward you.

PRAYER

Praying is a key step to successful work. To pray simply means speaking and listening to God or the higher power that you believe in. If you are persistent enough to pray every day, even if it's just for two minutes, you'll start to recognize many shifts. The power of praying will shift you to a higher level of consciousness. You'll start to become more aware of your mindset, your energy, and the rituals and spells that you pick to do. You'll see the growth in your spiritual development increase, and most of all, you'll start to recognize the prayers that became reality. Pray every day. The prayers that you say, think, or even write down as your intentions will be heard by the higher power that you believe. Plus, your ancestors and spirit guides that are there to assist you along your life journey will hear your prayers.

SAINTS AND SPIRITS

In the rootwork tradition, working with the spirit world is an integral part of the practice. You can call on aid from saints and spirits; there's no limit to the number of people who have transitioned to the spirit world or to deities and supernatural principles of the divine. You may seek help from any spiritual beings if you have that connection. It also depends on your spiritual belief system. Not all rootworkers work with the same spirits. Still, in essence, we all can connect and receive assistance from divine forces to achieve our intentions.

The connection started many generations ago, when Africans were taken and brought to different parts of the world, particularly the United States, and a complete transformation happened. Religion was one of many areas they were forced to conform to a new reality. They were not allowed to practice their own religious beliefs and spiritual traditions. They suffered tremendously while being forced to practice a new religion.

Eventually, African spirits were syncretized with Catholic saints to keep African spirituality hidden from the oppressors. Thankfully, a combination of Christianity and ceremonial practices imbued with African rituals and traditions developed. These practices helped in maintaining African culture, rituals, and traditions. Now, we see an increase of the African diaspora worldwide, and many individuals within the diaspora have a connection to rootwork practices, African religions, and spirituality.

Currently, many individuals continue to honor both an African deity and its associated saint. And many individuals throughout the world hide their religious and spiritual beliefs, even from their family and friends. Some come from a religious background, where they may fear that family members will not understand why they practice a certain spirituality or have the desire to learn about other beliefs. If you want to branch out and learn about other religions and spiritualities, know that it's okay. Being informed and gaining knowledge is great. As human beings, we have free will. We have the ability to make our own choices. So, moving forward, continue to make informed decisions that will only serve your highest good.

Be patient as you practice and develop a relationship with your ancestors, deities, spirits, and guides. If you are not aware of their presence already, you will learn about it with time. As a rootworker with a multicultural background and beliefs, I grew up directing my prayers and specific petitions to my ancestors and God. I also personally work with very specific neteru, or spirits from ancient Kemet (Egypt), orishas, and saints.

SAINTS AND SPIRITS LIST AND ASSOCIATIONS

AFRICAN SPIRITS

The African spirits, or orishas, originate from the cultural home of the Yoruba people in West Africa. They are also associated with Haitian Vodou and Louisiana voodoo spirits. They can be used to assist you with rituals, spells, and spiritual journey.

ELEGBA: The messenger orisha and the gatekeeper of all doors.

Also known as: Ellegua, Eshu, and Legba

Altar: Placement is behind the front door, in a cabinet, or outdoors.

Colors: black and red

Day: Monday

Favorite foods: candy, corn, and rum

Number: 3

Planet: Mercury

Symbol: stick

OBATALA: The orisha of justice, peace, and truth.

Also known as: Batala, Blanc Dani, and Oxala

Altar: Placement is higher than a normal altar height.

Colors: silver and white

Day: Sunday

Favorite foods: black-eyed peas, coconut, and pears

Number: 8

Planet: Jupiter

Symbol: dove and staff

OGUN: The orisha of metal, healing blood diseases, and war.

Also known as: Ogu and Ogum

Altar: Placement is behind the front door.

Colors: black and green

Day: Tuesday

Favorite foods: berries, meat, and nuts

Number: 3 and 4

Planet: Pluto and Saturn

Symbol: machete

OSHUN: The orisha of divine femininity, fertility, marriage, and women's health.

Also known as: Erzulie, Ochun, and Oxum

Altar: Placement is in the bedroom or kitchen area.

Colors: green, orange and yellow

Day: Thursday

Favorite foods: cinnamon, honey, oranges, and pumpkins

Number: 5

Planet: Venus

Symbol: fans, mirrors, and shells

OYA: The orisha of magick and protector of cemeteries, thunder, wind, and rebirth.

Also known as: Ayida-Weddo, Olla, and Yansa

Altar: Placement is in a fitness room, library, office, or study room.

Colors: green, orange, and yellow

Day: Thursday

Favorite foods: cinnamon, honey, oranges, and pumpkins

Number: 9

Planet: Venus

Symbol: fans, mirrors, and shells

SHANGO: The orisha of thunderbolt and justice.

Also known as: Chango and Xango

Altar: Placement is near a fireplace or living room with a fireplace.

Colors: red and white

Day: Friday

Favorite foods: corn and yams

Number: 6

Planet: Mars

Symbol: double axe

YEMONJA: The orisha of motherhood, pregnant women, and protection.

Also known as: Yemoja, Agwe, Imanje, La Balianne, and Yemaya

Altar: Placement is in the bathroom, bedroom, or children's room.

Colors: blue, silver, and white

Day: Thursday

Favorite foods: corn, molasses, and watermelon

Number: 7

Planet: Neptune

Symbol: conch shell and gourd rattle

RELIGIOUS FIGURES AND SAINTS

SANTO NIÑO: Patron of travelers and prisoners, and protection from danger.

Also known as: Santo Niño de Atocha and Santo Niño de Cebu

Syncretized with: Elegba

OUR LADY OF CHARITY: Patron of miners and protection.

Also known as: Mother of Charity and Virgin of Charity

Syncretized with: Oshun

OUR LADY OF MERCY: Patron of protection and shelter.

Also known as: Madonna of Mercy and Mother of Mercy

Syncretized with: Obatala

SAINT ANTHONY: Patron of returning lost items, of small requests, and of the poor.

Also known as: St. Antony and St. Anthony of Padua

Syncretized with: Ogun

SAINT BARBARA: Patron of architects, artillerymen, and miners.

Also known as: Great Martyr Barbara

Syncretized with: Shango

SAINT CATHERINE: Patron of scholars and sudden death.

Also known as: St. Catherine of Siena

Syncretized with: Oya

SAINT GEORGE: Patron of agricultural workers, farmers, and shepherds.

Also known as: George of Lydda

Syncretized with: Ogun

SAINT MICHAEL: Patron of protection in general, plus military personnel, police offers, and sailors.

Also known as: Archangel Michael

Syncretized with: Elegba

SAINT PETER: Patron of fisherman, locksmiths, popes, and ship builders.

Also known as: Peter the Apostle, Simon, Simon Peter.

Syncretized with: Ogun

SAINT THERESA: Patron of people with HIV, missionaries, and the sick.

Also known as: Therese of Lisieux

Syncretized with: Oya

SAINT MARY: Patron of all humanity and protection.

Also known as: Mother Mary, Mother of Jesus, Virgin Mary

Syncretized with: Yemonja

CHAPTER 12

PETITIONS

Words naturally exert a force of energy that can influence circumstances of any matter. The words we use attract, control, help, and make an influential impact for anyone that can use them. Allow yourself some time to meditate and contemplate your intentions in your sacred space or in front of your altar. This process may take place anywhere, but remember to find an area free from distractions.

I like to go out for a nature walk or sit on the beach facing the ocean to allow all of my senses the opportunity to feel energized and have a grounding experience. You can often attain more clarity and certainty after doing an activity that brings you joy. Capture the moment afterward when your vibration is on a higher level and write down the words you choose as your intentions. Remember, do not rush the process, even if it may take you some time to focus on your innermost desires and goals.

If speaking freely comes easier than writing, consider a voice recorder, or take a video of yourself. Afterward, replay it, write down your words, and revise them if needed. Choose your words wisely because this is the first step to manifestation. Next, write your intentions on your petition paper. Recite your words of power and feel the energy rise. Speaking the words of your soul aloud will uplift your energy even more; plus, your faith and hope will renew every time.

Following the rootwork tradition, write your petition on a brown piece of paper carefully torn into a shape of a square, circle, or heart. Rip the shape from the paper by hand on all sides, then proceed with writing your intentions down on the paper with the proper writing tools that fit your intentions. (For instance, if you're looking to increase matters of love in your life, use a pen that will only be used for love matters and speak your intentions into it.) Remember, you must be clear and precise with your desires and goals.

WRITING PETITIONS

Remember, positive thinking while writing your intentions increases the success rate and manifestation of your desires and goals.

A written petition may include the following:

* A name including another person's name next to it.

Example: Malachi Minor and Noa Smith

✳ A name crossing and covering your written goal.

Example: Write your intention: "Money, come to me now." Then write your name over your intention to increase the success rate of money coming to you.

✳ A name (person, place, or thing) crossing and covering an image (person, place, or thing).

Example: Choose an image that represents your desires (e.g., love). Then write your name over it to have it come true.

✳ A name (person, place, or thing) crossing and covering another name (person, place, or thing).

Example: If you wish to have someone come back to you, write that person's name and then write your name over it.

* A name written in the center and the intention written in the form of sentences, affirmations, or a prayer circling the name.

  Example: Write your name in the center. Next, write your intention around it. For example, "Money, come to me now from all directions and forms."

* A name written several times in a row (3, 5, 7, or 9 times or more). In my family tradition, we combine the power of numbers with how many times we write the name. The chosen name will depend on who the intention is for. Write your name or someone else's name several times.

  Example:

Bobbie Rae
Bobbie Rae
Bobbie Rae
Bobbie Rae
Bobbie Rae
Bobbie Rae
Bobbie Rae
Bobbie Rae
Bobbie Rae

* A paragraph clearly stating your goal.

  Example: I am ready to accept success into my life. I am worthy of abundance in all forms. Money, come to me now from all directions. I am valuable and deserving of happiness, optimal health, and wealth. I am ready for all blessings to come to me now.

* A prayer you've written yourself.

   Example: Divine, I call on you to intercede into my prayer. I ask for your assistance in receiving endless blessings from all directions and forms. I pray that the right help comes at the right time. Thank you for hearing my prayer.

* A well-known prayer.

   Examples: Our Father, Hail Mary, the Prayer to Archangel Michael, or orisha prayers.

* Affirmations in the form of individual words or sentences.

   Example: I am worthy of success, abundance in all forms, and joy.

* One to two sentences describing your intentions.

   Example: Money and success, come to me now in all shapes and forms. Success is mine now.

* One word to a few words.

   Example 1: Success.
   Example 2: Money, come to me now.

* A prayer to an ancestor, angel, deity, saint, or spiritual guide.

    Example: Dear Archangel Michael, I ask that you intercede into my prayer. I pray to have your constant assistance with protection. Please shield my family from harm, psychic attacks, and negative energies.

* A combination of the above.

    Example: Oshun, I call on you to intercede into my prayer. Please attract a new love to me that will fit my highest good. I am ready and worthy of new love now.

TYPES OF PAPER AND INK

In the beginning of this chapter, I shared the tradition of using a portion of a brown bag to write the desired petition. In addition to using commercialized papers, making homemade recycled paper out of bank statements or using paper from bank institutions for money rituals is ideal. The bank statements and other documents, such as deposit slips, hold the energy of the banking institution, which makes it a top material to have for money rituals. Using cards, notes, and other forms of documents given by specific people are also ideal for specific intentions that relate to that particular individual. For urgent matters, the use of construction paper, sticky notes, or notebook paper may be used for petition paper.

Here is a list of paper types:

- * Brown paper bag
- * Homemade recycled paper
- * Parchment paper
- * Rice paper
- * Soybean paper
- * Sugar bag

COLOR, INK, AND PEN TYPES

Color, ink, and pen types are very important with petition writing because of the additional energy they give to the ritual. The best advice given to me by an ancestor is to designate certain inks and pens only for the use of petition writing and rituals.

In my tradition, we are very specific with the materials that we use, especially with the type of pens. The purpose of the intention plus the type of petition paper will determine which pen to use. For instance, if your intention is to hex someone, black ink might suffice. If your intention is to draw love toward you or to deepen an existing relationship, pink and/or red would be the right choice as we associate these colors with love and relationships.

The goal is to produce a smooth, graceful flow from the beginning to the end of writing a petition. I love using fountain pens, ballpoint or felt-tip of specific color, and colored pencils. I also use a blade passed down through the generations to inscribe petitions into candles for rituals. For urgent matters or if you would rather not use pens, pencils, crayons, or paint may be used as a replacement.

Here is a list of pen types (available online) and their uses:

* Ballpoint pen
* Felt-tip pen
* Fountain pen
* Gel pen
* Marker
* Quill pen
* Rollerball pen

Use the proper ink type and color that match your intentions and goals. If the specific color or type of ink is not available, use the color black. Making your own ink is also ideal because it'll enhance the quality of energy that you imbue into your petition writing. Also, using natural dyes from fruits, herbs, roots, and vegetables is best.

Here is a list of the top ink types (available online) and their uses:

* Bat's blood (used for spells involving hexing, cursing, and binding)
* Dove's blood (used for spells involving romantic love)
* Dragon's blood (used for spells involving protection, love, potency, and cleansing)

Here is a list of the most common colors:

* Black for petitions relating to manifesting goals, protection, and releasing negative energies.

* Green for petitions relating to abundance, employment, family, money, and success.
* Pink for petitions relating to friendship, happiness, romance, love, and self-love.
* Purple for petitions relating to domination, loyalty, power, psychic abilities, and spirituality.
* Red for petitions relating to attraction, desires, love, passion, and relationships.

TOP 3 PETITIONS AND INSTRUCTIONS

Here are instructions for personal handwritten petitions pertaining to love. The petition formats may be modified to fit other intentions for matters of healing, money, or spirituality.

LOVE PETITION 1

Billy Jean 01/01/70 Las Vegas, NV	Joe Black 02/02/60 Primm, CA

1. Choose the desired petition paper, pen, and ink type.

2. Write your full birth name, your date of birth under your name, and the city and state of birth under your date of birth.

3. Write the other person's full birth name, their date of birth (you may use astrological signs if date of birth is unknown) under their name, and the city and state of birth under DOB.

LOVE PETITION 2

There are 3 variations of the Love Petition 2. Chose the one that calls out to you the most.

Variation 1

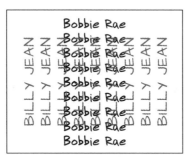

1. Choose the desired petition paper, pen, and ink type.

2. In the center of the petition paper (to give you enough space to write this petition), write the person's full name nine times in the color black.

3. Turn the paper clockwise and write your full name nine times in capital letters in the color red, crossing their name each time.

Variation 2

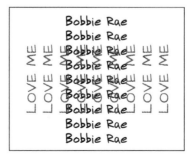

1. Choose the desired petition paper, pen, and ink type.

2. In the center of the petition paper (to give you enough space to write this petition), write the person's full name plus a desire, such as "Come back to me," nine times in the color black.

3. Turn the paper clockwise and write your full name nine times in capital letters in the color red, crossing their name each time.

Variation 3

1. Choose the desired petition paper, pen, and ink type.

2. In the center of the petition paper (to give you enough space to write this petition), write the person's full name nine times in the color black.

3. Turn the paper clockwise and write a desire, such as "Love me," nine times in capital letters in the color red, crossing their name each time.

LOVE PETITIONS 3

1. Follow one of the variations from Love Petition 2.

2. With Petition 2 in the center, now write in cursive without lifting your pen from the paper a command that you want the other person to do for you around that petition. Some examples are:

* Come to me now
* Commit to me now
* Love me now

3. Do not cross any T's or dot any I's until you connect your last letter with the first initial letter.

4. Lastly, draw a complete circle in black to seal the petition.

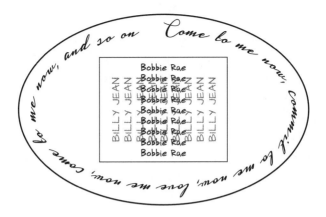

FOLDING TECHNIQUE

It is tradition to fold your petition a specific way. I will share the main two techniques.

ATTRACTION

If your intention is to attract something toward you, this may be the technique for you. After you finish writing down your petition, take the top of the paper and fold it in half toward you. Then turn the paper clockwise and fold it a second time toward you. Lastly, turn the paper clockwise for the third time and fold it toward you. Proceed with using your petition for candle work, a mojo bag, a jar spell, or other rootwork spells.

DISPEL/MOVE AWAY

If your intention is to dispel something away from you or someone else, this may be the technique for you. After you finish writing down your petition, take the bottom of the paper and fold it in half away from you. Then turn the paper clockwise and fold it a second time away from you. Lastly, turn the paper clockwise for the third time and fold it away from you. Proceed with using your petition for candle work, a mojo bag, a jar spell, or other rootwork spells.

CHAPTER 13

※

THE ASTROLOGICAL COLOR CHART

※

Astrological colors represent a spiritual connection to you based on your astrological sun sign. Astrological colors are used for candles or any other magickal tools when you are performing your own personal ritual work. Make or pick a candle made in the associated color that correlates to your astrological sign. Place it in the center of your altar or dedicated sacred space for your rituals and spells.

ASTROLOGICAL BIRTH SIGN	ASTROLOGICAL COLORS
Aquarius: January 20 to Feb 18	Blue and green
Pisces: February 19 to March 20	Green and white
Aries: March 21 to April 19	White and pink
Taurus: April 20 to May 20	Red and yellow
Gemini: May 21 to June 20	Red and blue
Cancer: June 21 to July 22	Green and brown
Leo: July 23 to Aug 22	Red and green
Virgo: August 23 to Sept 22	Gold and black
Libra: September 23 to Oct 22	Black and blue
Scorpio: October 23 to Nov 21	Brown and black
Sagittarius: November 22 to Dec 21	Gold and red
Capricorn: December 22 to Jan 19	Red and brown

AQUARIUS: January 20 to February 18
Colors: Blue and green

The luckiest day of the week for you to perform personal rituals and spells is Wednesday. Mercury rules Wednesday, which is symbolic for communication, intelligence, and vigilance. It's a day with themes of balance, harmony, and moderation. Wednesday is a great day to reflect upon past accomplishments as well as future goals.

PISCES: February 19 to March 20
Colors: Green and white

The luckiest day of the week for you to perform personal rituals and spells is Thursday. Jupiter rules Thursday, which is symbolic for ambition, expansion, and personal growth. This day also represents abundance, finances, and protection.

ARIES: March 21 to April 19
Colors: White and pink

The luckiest day of the week for you to perform personal rituals and spells is Tuesday. Mars rules Tuesday, which is symbolic for determination, exerting healthy amounts of energy, and power.

TAURUS: April 20 to May 20
Colors: Red and yellow

The luckiest day of the week for you to perform personal rituals and spells is Friday. Venus rules Friday, which is a symbolic time for celebration and love.

GEMINI: May 21 to June 20
Colors: Red and blue

The luckiest day of the week for you to perform personal rituals and spells is Wednesday. Mercury rules Wednesday, which is symbolic for communication, intelligence, and vigilance. It's a day with themes of balance, harmony, and moderation. Wednesday is a great day to reflect upon past accomplishments as well as future goals.

CANCER: June 21 to July 22
Colors: Green and brown

The luckiest day of the week for you to perform personal rituals and spells is Monday. The Moon rules Monday, which is symbolic for cycles, emotions, and secrets. Monday is a great day of creating, starting new projects, and setting new intentions.

LEO: July 23 to August 22
Colors: Red and green

The luckiest day of the week for you to perform personal rituals and spells is Sunday. The Sun rules Sunday, which is symbolic of energy and existence. Sunday is a great day of inspiration and strength.

VIRGO: August 23 to September 22
Colors: Gold and black

The luckiest day of the week for you to perform personal rituals and spells is Wednesday. Mercury rules Wednesday, which is symbolic for communication, intelligence, and vigilance. It's a day with themes of balance, harmony, and moderation. Wednesday is a great day to reflect upon past accomplishments as well as future goals.

LIBRA: September 23 to October 22
Colors: Black and blue

The luckiest day of the week for you to perform personal rituals and spells is Friday. Venus rules Friday, which is a symbolic time for celebration and love.

SCORPIO: October 23 to November 21
Colors: Brown and black

The luckiest day of the week for you to perform personal rituals and spells is Tuesday. Mars rules Tuesday, which is symbolic for determination, exerting healthy amounts of energy, and power.

SAGITTARIUS: November 22 to December 21
Colors: Gold and red

The luckiest day of the week for you to perform personal rituals and spells is Thursday. Jupiter rules Thursday, which is symbolic for ambition, expansion, and personal growth. This day also represents abundance, finances, and protection.

CAPRICORN: December 22 to January 19
Colors: Red and brown

The luckiest day of the week for you to perform personal rituals and spells is Saturday. Saturn rules Capricorn, which is symbolic for power and structure. This day also represents accomplishments and productivity.

PART FOUR

ADVANCED MAGICK

CHAPTER 14

CANDLE MAGICK

I can vividly recall peeking along the side of the kitchen wall or tiptoeing over the countertop as a child to see what magick my dad was conjuring up during the night. It is in my bloodline to create magick, and as a result, my curiosity around conjuring only grew within me over the years. At the tender age of eight, I melted red, blue, and purple pieces of wax on a white pillar candle alongside my encouraging dad as he was making candles for his clients and for us. Candles meant the world to us; we used them daily in our home for rituals. Our way of using candles has helped not only my family but also others that we advised to reach their goals. With a childhood filled with illuminating and enjoyable experiences surrounded by candles, I was thankful to grow up in a way that embraced free thinking, spirituality, and hoodoo.

Candle magick rituals and spells is one of the easiest forms of magick to learn and incorporate into your practice. As a descendant candle maker, my family and ancestors gave me the blessing to carry on the craft so that I can assist others on their spiritual journey during this lifetime. The negative stigma that our mainstream world has toward hoodoo candles has been destructive, passed down throughout generations and continuing to create fear for others by labeling anything that is a direct relation to Africa or African American traditions and cultures as dangerous. As the media continues to deliver this false information in 2021, I am here to tell you that if one chooses to use candles in a negative matter to wish harm upon someone, that is their own doing. Do not assume that everything "negative" or "black magick" is a direct relation to voodoo or hoodoo. Release the stigma; understand that it is now time to relearn the truth and rekindle the light within your own being. I will show you that hoodoo candles and candle magick in general are spiritual tools for obtaining your goals in a positive way.

The magickal power derived from candle magick comes from your intentions. The color of the candle is important as well as the incense you choose and the pairing of the herbs and oils, all combined in a ritual. The ritual may be very complex, with the use of multiple candles, or very simple, with the use of just one candle.

In my practice, I mainly use freestanding candles like pillar and image candles.

Here are the main candle types:

* Pillar candles are usually shaped like a cylinder and can range in size.

* Image candles are candles that are shaped as a person, place, or thing.

* Tealight candles are 40 mm cylindrical candles inside of thin metal or plastic holders.

* Taper candles are long cylindrical candles that are usually hand dipped and can range in size.

* Candles in glass jars range in size.

* Floating candles are shallow candles that are shaped and made a specific way to float on any water surface. Do not get the wick wet or else you won't be able to light it.

The image and pillar candles that I make and use help me focus directly on the intentions more effectively. For example, when the intention I'm setting is to increase my luck with money, I use the green elephant candle to do so. Both elephants and the color green represent good luck. However, your intentions and prayers are important factors with candle magick, and you can still succeed with using other forms of candles such as a tealight candle or small 4-inch taper candle.

Candles anointed with oils, powders, herbs, and roots intensify their powers. Remember, your state of mind is still the most important factor of your divine power. The importance of positive thinking while burning the candles ensures the success of the ritual and the manifestation of your goals and desires.

The power of burning candles initiates an altered state of consciousness. Reflect on the last time you had a candlelight dinner. How did the energy feel in your environment? Did another individual accompany you during this time? How was their energy? Were the energies calming and relaxing or filled with passion and love? What about a time you lit a candle while taking a relaxing bath or during a meditation practice? We know that candles can produce different energies depending on the conditions. From influencing to nurturing to even resolving issues, the glowing magick of a candle can alter the state of consciousness for many.

With practice and repetition, you will become familiar with the magickal associations of colors, smoke interpretations, days of the week, flame interpretations, and more. There are varieties of candles that fit any intention you may need or want to attract into your life or away from your life. A candle can be any color that you desire, but if possible, I would recommend you match your intentions to the magickal association of colors (see chart to follow). When in doubt, trust your intuition for assistance. Your inner guidance is very powerful.

The following is a chart of frequently used colors:

COLOR	MAGICKAL ASSOCIATIONS
GREEN	Abundance, Earth Element, Employment, Fertility, Good Luck, Healing, Health, Heart Chakra, Money, Nature Magick, Prosperity, Success
RED	Courage, Energy, Fiery, Fire Element, Health, Life, Love, Loyalty, Lust, Magnetism, Passion, Power, Relationships, Root Chakra, Sexual Desires, Strength
YELLOW	Action, Air Magick, Communication, Confidence, Clairvoyance, Creativity, Inspiration, Manifesting Thoughts, Mental Clarity, Releasing, Solar Plexus Chakra, Success, Unity, Universal Love
ORANGE	Activation Energy, Adaptability, Attraction, Education, Enthusiasm, Friendship, Happiness, Intellect, Joy, Self-Control, Sacral Chakra, Stimulation, Strength, Success
PINK	Affection, Family, Femininity, Friendship, Self-Love, Happiness, Harmony, Heart Chakra, Honor, Peace, Romance, Spiritual Awakening
BLUE	Communication, Harmony in the Home, Health, Justice, Honesty, Meditation, Peace, River and Sea Magick, Serenity, Throat Chakra, Water Element, Wisdom, Wishes
PURPLE	Ambition, Awakening, Awareness, Confidence, Domination, Empowerment Intuition, Healing, Leadership, Power, Pride, Spirits, Spirituality, Third Eye Chakra, Tranquility, Wisdom

BLACK	Banishing, Breakup, Good Luck, Separation, Protection against Evil Spirits, Protection against Negative Energies, Removing Spells, Spirit Communication
BROWN	Animal Healing, Balance, Concentration, Earth and Nature Magick, Uncertainty, Intuitive Communication, Justice, Law, Order, Stability
WHITE	Aura Healing, Altar, Ancestors, Blessings, Cleansing, Crown Chakra, Destroying Negative Energies, House Blessing, Meditation, Purification, Peace, Truth, Self-Blessings, Spirit Communication, Spirituality, Wishes

As you choose a candle to use, ensure that you cleanse it if needed. Depending on where the candle comes from, it is important to know that if it traveled quite a ways, it may have been touched by a number of people during transit to the store or directly to you. The candles that we make at Hoodoo Goddess LLC are carefully prepared with the individual's intentions in mind. All candles receive blessings, energetic healing, and love. We suggest that our customers and clients cleanse their candles upon arrival if they intuitively feel called to do so. Then proceed to charging the candle.

VOTIVE CANDLES

These instructions are simple to follow, and the materials are easy to find at your local arts and crafts store or in my shop. You have

the option to buy votive candle molds or simply use disposable
Dixie Cups. This is a beginner-level candle recipe.

1 candle and soap scale

1 pound wax (paraffin, soy, or beeswax)

1 small candle-making pitcher

10 to 14 drops candle fragrance (optional)

1 color dye chip or color crayon (optional)

1 medium to large saucepan

1 glass thermometer for candle making

1 silicone spatula

6 votive candle molds or (3-ounce) disposable paper Dixie cups

6 cotton wicks for votive wicks

6 clothespins

6 votive candleholder

1. Use the scale to make sure you have one pound of wax. Pour the wax into a small candle-melting pitcher. Add your candle fragrance and color dye now, if using.

2. Use the double boiler method by placing the filled pitcher inside a saucepan filled with 2 inches of water. Heat on low only until the heat is up to 150°F. Use your glass thermometer to moderate the temperature. Using the spatula, stir slowly, allowing the wax to melt down with a silicone spatula.

3. After the wax is completely melted, turn off the heat and pour the wax at a temperature of 130°F to 140°F. Fill each Dixie cup or votive mold to three-fourths full.

4. Put the pitcher with the remaining wax back in the saucepan. Place the cotton wick at the end of the clothespins. Position the clothespin so that the bottom of the wick is resting at the center of the cup or mold. Ensure that the cotton wick is positioned properly at the center of each cup or mold. The wick needs to be upright.

5. Reheat the remaining wax, if needed, at the same temperature. Allow the poured candles to cool for at least 10 minutes.

6. Slowly remove the clothespin holder and pour the remaining wax to the brim of the cup or mold.

7. Allow the candle to set for at least 24 hours. Remove your new candle by peeling away the Dixie cup or turning the mold upside down to pop out the candle easily. Trim the wick if needed and place the votive candle inside a candleholder before doing your candle ritual.

CHARGING YOUR CANDLE

1. Hold your candle in your hand.

2. Start with a prayer and recite a positive affirmation or your intentions as you "charge" it with your energy. The support you ask for may be from your ancestors, angels, deities, God (the Divine, Higher Power, Spirit, etc.), Goddess, orishas, or other spirit beings.

3. As you are holding your candle, ask for spiritual intervention from the Divine, your ancestors, and spirit guides. Your personal power will release to the universe and to those that you ask for direct support.

4. Place your candle on your altar or on a clean table. Then position your hands over the candle, forming a triangle with your fingers and thumbs. Keep the candle in the center of your triangle.

5. Continue to visualize that which you desire as you say your intentions or prayer.

6. When you are done, gently tap the candle on the table three times to signal that your intention is sealed.

THE IMPORTANCE OF TIME

The following list of frequently used options can help you prepare for your candle ritual:

* Light the candle in one session.
  * Light the candle until it burns out completely on its own.

* Light the candle for a specific amount of time each day.
  * Pick a specific time each day to light the candle.

* Light the candle on specific days only.
  * Pick specific days to light the candles.

* Light the candle during specific moon phases.

- Pick a specific moon phase, whether it is the new moon, waxing moon, full moon, waning moon (or dark moon) to light the candles.

✳ Burn the candle on specific days of the week only.

- Pick a specific day of the week to light your candle. Each day of the week has a symbolic association. Some associations are related to the planets, astrological signs, orishas, deities etc. (see Chapter 13 to determine your luckiest day of the week according to your astrological sign, and Days of the Week for associations connected to specific days.)

DAYS OF THE WEEK

In candle magick, choosing a specific day of the week will enhance the energies of your intentions, aligning them with additional associations.

✳ **Sunday**

- Sunday is ruled by the Sun.
- Sunday is associated with achievement, authority figures, business, career, employment, spirituality, success, and wealth.

✳ **Monday**

- Monday is ruled by the Moon.
- Monday is associated with dreams, cycles, emotions, family, intuition, spirit work, and psychic work.

✳ Tuesday

- Tuesday is ruled by Mars.
- Tuesday is associated with power, dealing with enemies, negative energies, relationships, sexuality, and war.

✳ Wednesday

- Wednesday is ruled by Mercury.
- Wednesday is associated with communication, healing, goals, and wisdom.

✳ Thursday

- Thursday is ruled by Jupiter.
- Thursday is associated with business, career, expansion, happiness, health, justice, luck.

✳ Friday

- Friday is ruled by Venus.
- Friday is associated with friendship, emotions, love, marriage, passion, romance, and sexual desires.

✳ Saturday

- Saturday is ruled by Saturn.
- Saturday is associated with ambition, business, health, protection, psychic attacks, and transformation.

THE MOON PHASE

Similar to the days of the week, the phases of the moon have their own associations and energies of power. Each phase lasts about three days. Light your candle under the specific moon phase to enhance and receive the extra energy boost from the moon.

The full moon phase occurs when the moon is biggest, brightest, round, and 100 percent visible. The moon energy is powerful for doing any type of rituals or spells for success and manifesting your intentions.

The waning moon phase occurs when you see the moon shaped as a crescent or C, with the light on the left side and the dark on the right side. This phase occurs after the full moon phase. The moon energy is powerful for doing rituals and spells for cleansing and releasing what no longer serves your highest good.

The new moon phase occurs when the moon is dark. This phase occurs after the waning moon phase. The moon energy is powerful for doing cleansing, divinations, and rituals that require a major transformation.

The waxing moon phase occurs when you see the moon shaped as a crescent or reverse C, with the light on the right side and the dark on the left side. This phase occurs after the new moon. The moon energy is powerful for doing rituals and spells for abundance, attraction, and setting new intentions and goals for growth.

FLAME MAGICK

Have you noticed during your candle magick rituals that your candles burn differently each time?

When doing your candle ritual or spells, you want to ensure that you are burning with candle fire safety in mind. Please review the following safety rules before proceeding to light any candles:

* Read the warning sign and instructions. Candles will have this on the label.

* Always remember to keep the candles away from any drafts, open windows or doors, air vents, fans, and heaters. Avoiding certain areas will help prevent rapid, uneven burning, flame flare-ups, and the flame traveling and catching things on fire.

* A draft may also influence and cause misinterpretations of the flames. If you find your flame in motion as if there is a draft, this may indicate some very important communication that you need to pay attention to in regard to your ritual or spell.

I personally believe that as you continue to burn your candles and develop a connection to your observations, you will understand the communication intuitively without effort. Just like anything else (pendulum, shells, tarot, oracle, runes, etc.), it may take some time to establish a partnership with your spiritual tools.

Each candle ritual set forth is powerful. The movement of the flame is filled with messages. These highly sensitive messages are released through sound, images, thoughts, and even channeling through the other senses, including the mind's eye, also known as the third eye.

You may notice each time you do a candle magick ritual that the flame burns differently each time. When performing candle rituals, keep a designated candle magick journal and pen nearby. Collect any vital information regarding the signs that may occur while watching the flame. Your interpretation may differ from someone else's interpretation, so keeping a record of your observations is very important to build a personalized book of flame interpretations. Use the information provided here as a basic guide.

CANDLE FLAME INTERPRETATION

Use this to help you determine the meaning of the strength/weakness of the flame.

* A strong steady flame may indicate a positive sign that the ritual is going smoothly.

* A strong and high flame may indicate rapid success without any interference of negative energies.

* A flame that moves as if there is a draft in the room may indicate that you need to pay close attention with all your senses ready to receive messages in the forms of visions, sounds, tastes, thoughts, scents, and so forth. This may be a sign of messages being delivered to you by the Divine, ancestors, spirit guides, angels, or deities that assist you.

* A flame that starts off weak, gradually strengthening in size and becoming a strong, solid flame may indicate that there was some resistance, but the barriers have been released and the candle ritual can move forward with positive results.

* A weak, sputtering flame may indicate resistance. You may need to replace this ritual or repeat a stronger one several times if the flame remains in this low state.

* A slow-burning flame may indicate the intention is not clear enough or it may take longer to manifest this specific intention. Take some time to reflect and listen to your thoughts. Were there any signs indicating that a spiritual cleanse or purification is needed in order to manifest this specific intention? Write down what comes to you automatically.

* A lump or knot that develops on the tip of the wick may indicate stubbornness or resistance.

FLAME DIRECTION INTERPRETATION

Use this to help you determine the meaning of the direction of the flame as it relates to the cardinal directions.

* A flame burning toward the north may indicate the occurrence of physical development. Immediate movement toward manifestation of the intention may occur.

* A flame burning toward the east may indicate the occurrence of mental development. Immediate psychological movement with the ritual may occur. Take this time to give deep thought about the motive behind the ritual. If the intention is carried on to manifestation, will it serve your highest good?

* A flame burning toward the south may indicate the occurrence of energy surrounding the intention of the ritual. Immediate change in the energy flow of the ritual may happen rapidly, but the success of the manifestation may be short term.

* A flame burning toward the west may indicate the occurrence of profound emotions. An immediate shift in your emotional state of awareness regarding the ritual may occur. You may need to repeat this ritual several times for it to manifest completely.

* A flame that alternates frequently from west to east may indicate indecisiveness or imbalances.

* A flame that favors one direction throughout the entire ritual, resulting in uneven wax flow, may indicate

unbalanced relationships in rituals pertaining to love, family, business, and self.

* A flickering and flaring flame may indicate several interpretations. Use your intuition to decipher which meaning resonates with you.

  • A flame that continuously flares up and down may indicate signs of possible obstacles.
  • A flame that continuously flares up and down may indicate an appearance of a spirit or spirits.
  • A flaring flame may indicate resistance from a rival.

* A flame that spirals upward may indicate that the people the ritual is intended for, whether it is you or others, are being affected immediately.

FLAME MOVEMENT INTERPRETATION

Use this to help you determine the meaning of the movement of the flame as it relates to multiple flames appearing or a flame that goes out and relights itself.

* A flame that constantly flares up may indicate obstacles. Please see Flame Direction Interpretation on page 207 for more details.

* A flame that goes out and relights itself slowly may indicate an individual working against you, but your ritual is fighting back.

* A flame that goes out and relights itself instantly may indicate an individual is intuitively aware of your ritual and may be resisting a positive outcome.

* A flame that relights itself after being put out properly to pause the ritual may indicate that the ritual wants to continue burning or may need additional candles to continue to burn for stronger assistance.

* A single flame that is accompanied by a new flame, making two flames in total, may indicate several interpretations. Use your intuition to decipher which meaning resonates with you.

  * Two flames may indicate a positive outcome.
  * Two flames may indicate a new partnership.
  * Two flames that later join as one may indicate a stronger bond or reconciliation.
  * A flame birthed out of wick ashes may indicate a rival or the need to be aware of another person's motives.
  * A flame with four or more flames resembling a fan may indicate the need to reexamine the intentions (reason) for the ritual.

* A single flame that is accompanied by two new flames, making three flames in total, may indicate a rival inference.

* A candle that falls over and causes a fire may indicate several interpretations. Use your intuition to decipher which meaning resonates with you.

- A candle that falls and causes a fire may indicate a negative outcome and may suggest there is a negative presence around you.

- A candle that falls and causes a fire may indicate the need to properly dispose of the candle immediately and cleanse the area, altar space, and yourself. Bless the area, set forth protection energies, and ask spirit guides to assist you with a spiritual protection ritual.

- A candle that falls with wax spills directed toward you, resulting in a fire, may indicate the beginning of a spiritual attack that was intercepted by your ritual and spirit guides. Properly dispose of the candle immediately and cleanse the area, altar space, and yourself. Bless the area, set forth protection energies, and ask spirit guides to assist you with your spiritual protection ritual. Then repeat the original ritual with a new blessed candle.

* When the top portion of a candle is on fire, including the flame, this may indicate a positive outcome.

TWO CANDLE FLAMES INTERPRETATION

When working with two candles, both flames provide several interpretations.

* If Candle A's flame is leaning toward Candle B's flame (or vice versa), this may indicate a stronger desirer for Candle B.

* If Candle A's flame is leaning away from Candle B (or vice versa), this may indicate indifferent feelings for Candle B.

* If Candle A's flame is leaning toward Candle B, and Candle B's flame is leaning away (or vice versa), this may indicate an unbalanced relation. Candle A desires Candle B. Candle B feels indifferent.

* If Candle A's and Candle B's flames are leaning toward each other, this may indicate equal desires for each other.

* If Candle A's and Candle B's flames are leaning away from each other, this may indicate indifferent feelings toward each other or that both are having issues from the past that haven't been resolved. In addition, ritual outcome may not be favorable for reconciliation.

* If Candle A has one flame and Candle B has one flame that develops a second flame from ash, this may indicate a love triangle, a rival, or an individual that has a stronger effect on Candle B.

* If Candle A's flame is larger than Candle B's flame (or vice versa), this may indicate that Candle A is the dominant one compared to Candle B.

FLAME SOUND INTERPRETATION

A crackling-sound, including sizzling, hissing, and popping, may indicate several interpretations. Use your intuition to decipher which meaning resonates with you.

* A soft crackling sound may indicate spirits in communication among each other or wanting to communicate with you regarding your request.

* A strong crackling sound may indicate the occurrence of arguments among those related to the ritual.

* A loud crackling sound may indicate someone working against you.

* A frequent crackling sound may indicate that someone with strong abilities is influencing the outcome of the ritual.

* An infrequent crackling sound may indicate peaceful thoughts regarding the ritual.

* A sizzling sound may indicate negativity energies being removed.

* A hissing sound may indicate delusion, or a possible rival speaking ill of you. It may indicate the serpent power energy rising within the individual or yourself. If you are unfamiliar with the serpent energy and feel an interest rising, conduct further research. Research the term "kundalini," or serpent energy.

* A popping sound may indicate a surprise that might occur before the ritual reaches completion.

* A candle that sparkles may indicate a positive outcome.

FLAME COLORS INTERPRETATION

A single-colored flame or an array of colors may indicate several interpretations. Use your intuition to decipher which meaning resonates with you.

* A vibrant red coloration of the flame may indicate an abundant flow of passion.

* A persistent amount of blue coloration of the flame may indicate spirit guides, specifically angels, assisting and protecting you. It may also indicate obstacles ahead.

* A rainbow coloration of the flame may indicate a correlation between the intention and energetic chakra energy and/or aura. Pay close attention to the prominent color(s) appearing to you.

SMOKE INTERPRETATION

Similar to the flame of the candle, the smoke that comes afterward is also important to pay attention to so that you can determine if there is a positive or negative outcome that may enter your life. Use the interpretations below to help you determine the meaning of the smoke.

* No smoke may indicate your ritual will be clear of any obstacles.

* White smoke may indicate several interpretations. Use your intuition to decipher which meaning resonates with you.

- White smoke may indicate a positive outcome; however, there may be obstacles.
- An excessive amount of white smoke in the beginning of the ritual, which subsides with a steady flame and the candle burning evenly, may indicate a positive outcome.
- An excessive amount of white smoke in the beginning of the ritual, with the candle burning unevenly, may indicate that the ritual may need to be repeated several times.
- Puffs of white smoke may indicate doubts surrounding intentions.
- Crackling, sizzling, hissing, or popping sounds followed by white smoke may indicate a positive outcome.

* Black smoke may indicate that the ritual is removing negative energy or there may be some obstacles ahead that will be cleared.

* Excessive smoke may indicate some interference that may occur but will subside at the end.

* Excessive smoke and fast burning may indicate a spiritual attack that was shielded by your ritual.

* Smoke without fire may indicate insecurities and doubts regarding the ritual.

* Smoke moving toward the west may indicate the occurrence of profound emotions within you. You may experience an immediate shift in emotional state and

awareness regarding the ritual. You may need to repeat or rethink the motive behind doing this ritual several times in order for it to manifest completely.

* Smoke moving toward the east may indicate the occurrence of mental development. An immediate psychological movement may occur with the ritual. Take this time to give deep thought about the motive behind the ritual. If the intention is carried on to manifestation, will it serve your highest good?

* Smoke that is constantly moving toward you may indicate that any obstacles pertaining to your intention will resolve.

* Smoke that gracefully flows toward you may indicate that your ritual will have a positive outcome.

* Smoke consistently moving away from you may indicate that any obstacles pertaining to your intention may remain. You may want to reexamine your intention and focus on prayer throughout the ritual.

WHEN A FLAME GOES OUT INTERPRETATION

A flame may go out for several reasons, excluding any candle malfunctions due to wick size or excessive use of oils, herbs, and minerals used on the wick or wax. When the flame goes out, take a moment to listen within yourself. Use your intuition to decipher which meaning for this occurrence resonates with you.

* Ritual should be discontinued due to a negative outcome.

* Someone is working a stronger candle spell against you and your spiritual protection barriers were penetrated.

* You are working against someone's free will, and the resistance is powerful.

* Reexamine your motives behind the ritual. Is it self-serving and not serving your highest good? Are you performing this particular ritual to do ill on someone? Take this time to reexamine your intentions.

If you are having a hard time determining which option best resonates with you, use a pendulum (divination tool) over the candle. Ask yes or no questions on what to do next or provide options and ask which of the options you should proceed with next.

* Properly dispose of the candle(s), herbs, and minerals used during the ritual in running water or at any crossroads closest to you. Cleanse the area, altar space, and yourself. Bless your area and set forth protection energies by asking the Divine to assist you with a spiritual protection ritual. Reexamine the intentions for the ritual and decide if you should continue with a different candle ritual or use the same type of candle.

* Take a moment to reexamine the intentions for the ritual and decide if a stronger prayer is needed. If so, cleanse the area, altar space, and yourself. Bless the area, set forth protection energies, and ask your spirit

guides to assist you with a spiritual protection ritual. You may also consider adding an additional candle (usually a white, black, or red/black candle, depending on the ritual) to support your candle ritual. Relight the candle immediately after cleansing and blessing, and recite stronger prayers, chants, affirmations, and/or intentions.

If you are unsure of what to do, cleanse the area, altar space, and yourself, dispose of the candle, and work with a different candle the next day. Upon awakening, write down the last dream that appeared to you. This will provide some additional information on what to do moving forward with a new candle ritual.

CHAPTER 15

RITUALS AND SPELLS

In the rootwork tradition, rituals and spells are at the heart and soul of the practice. Each has a purpose and goal to achieve something more for yourself and others. There is no limit to the type of ritual or spell you do because eventually, everything you do, from cleaning your home with herbs to anointing your body with oils to meditating with candles, becomes a whole way of being. It's the hoodoo lifestyle.

Magickal and spiritual workings for yourself and others go out to the energetic world to attract and bring back a sign, movement, and outcome. The influences of each item boost the power of the magick and increase the chance for positive results. We always reap what we sow when it comes to rootwork. If you put forth high-vibrating energy with your work, then that energy will come back. There may be times when the harvest is delayed, but rest assured that everything meant for you or someone else will come in divine timing.

If you use your rituals and spells to harm someone, be prepared to shield yourself from that energy coming back. Be mindful and thoughtful of the abilities and tools that you use. Whenever you perform a new ritual or spell, try it yourself first before doing it for others. Remember, it takes time to practice your craft and harness those energies. By going through Parts 1 to 3 of this book, you have built a good foundation around what type of rituals and spells will work best for you, depending on your circumstances.

DAYS OF THE WEEK

Each day of the week carries its own energy. Each day corresponds with actions that will intensify the powers of your rituals and spells. Choose a day that best fits your desires and goals. See Days of the Week on page 201.

VENUS TIMES

Another wonderful way to align your rituals and spells pertaining to all matters of love is to align your day and time with planet Venus. In addition to love, Venus influences marriage, comfort, luxury, beauty, prosperity, and happiness. The planet can also affect your creativity and fill you with the divine feminine energy.

There are planetary hours in which each traditional planet in astrology rules and is at its peak. The hours listed below are the ruling hours of Venus. Use the days and times below to begin your rituals and spells so that you experience a greater outcome of what Venus has to offer.

Sunday: 2:00 a.m., 9:00 a.m., 4:00 p.m., and 11:00 p.m.

Monday: 6:00 a.m., 1:00 p.m., and 8:00 p.m.

Tuesday: 3:00 a.m., 10:00 a.m., 5:00 p.m., and 12:00 p.m.

Wednesday: 7:00 a.m., 2:00 p.m., and 9:00 p.m.

Thursday: 4:00 a.m., 11:00 a.m., and 6:00 p.m.

Friday: 1:00 a.m., 8:00 a.m., 3:00 p.m., and 11:00 p.m.

Saturday: 5:00 a.m., 12:00 p.m., and 7:00 p.m.

MOJO BAGS

Mojo bags are also known as charm bags, conjure bags, and gris-gris bags, as mentioned on page 22.

Depending on where you are from, a mojo bag is also known as a medicine bag. Regardless of the name, they are traditionally made with a cloth drawstring bag or sachet. The standard material is flannel, and the size runs about 2 x 3 inches long.

Typically, a mojo bag is prepared at your altar with personal matters such as hair, nails, or a piece of clothing that belonged to you and/or another person, and a photo. Additionally, consecrated herbs, minerals, oils, a petition, and other ingredients and materials such as amulets, crystals, stones, or talismans may be added to the bag. As you carefully pick your items, you direct your prayer and command the instructions for each item to attract specific influences, such as money, new love, and protection from spiritual attacks.

I suggest listening to Muddy Waters's song, "Got My Mojo Workin'," to give you an idea of how significant a mojo bag was when Muddy made the song. This song about mojo bags was also one of my favorite songs to listen to at Grandma Mary Ree's house. It's a nostalgic feeling of my childhood and growing up with rootworkers.

Here's an easy and quick formula for how to use a mojo bag, specifically for attracting new money toward you.

NEW MONEY MOJO BAG

Green pen

Personal matter:
blank check
business card
photo

A few drops of Fast-Money Oil (see page 133)

Red cloth drawstring bag

Cinnamon powder or stick

Parchment paper

Lodestone (green)

A pinch of patchouli (dried)

Magnetic sand

A pinch of peppermint (dried)

Directions

1. Pray over all of your ingredients and materials before preparing your mojo bag for partnership.

2. Write a business command with your green pen on your parchment paper or business card. Some examples are:

* New customers, come to me now!
* I will have ten new patients per day!
* I will receive $1,000 of sales on a daily basis!

3. Next, anoint the four corners of the business card with money oil.

4. Put a small amount of cinnamon over the petition on the business card and place it inside the bag.

5. Write the amount of money that you need with the green pen on the check.

6. Next, anoint the 4 corners and center of the check with money oil. Fold the check toward you three times and place it inside your bag.

7. Put a small amount of peppermint herb over the check and business card.

8. Write a money command or money affirmation on your photo three times. Some examples are:

- ✳ I accept and embrace wealth in my life.
- ✳ I am skilled at creating assets that make me wealthy.

9. Anoint the four corners of your photo with money oil, then place it inside the bag.

10. Next, place the green lodestone inside the bag.

11. Put a small amount of patchouli over the lodestone.

12. Anoint the bag with money oil and then tie it up.

13. Put the bag in a clean, dark, and dry place where no one will touch it for seven days.

14. On the seventh day, take it out and carry it with you in your pocket, in your bra, or pinned inside your clothing.

15. Recite "money will come to me," say your chosen prayer, or recite Psalm 23.

16. Anoint your mojo bag with money oil or add magnetic sand to it and for it to continue working for you.

HONEY JARS

In the rootwork tradition, honey jar spells assist with attracting a positive outcome toward you and sweetening up that outcome. These types of spells are for all matters of love, including self-love, battling court cases, career aspirations, money drawing, and more. Like the mojo bag formula, you can add various ingredients such as crystals, herbs, minerals, personal matters, petitions, photos, roots, and stones to the honey jar. Once you are done adding your elements inside the honey jar, you will add a candle on top of the lid to burn for multiple days. The candle plus the combination of every consecrated ingredient added inside the jar will enhance the spell to a higher level. The two primary functions of a honey jar spell are to attract and sweeten up.

For those who are vegan, you can substitute honey with agave, molasses, or sugar. Brown and white sugar are the best options. Honey and sugar jar spells are some of my favorite types of spells. Even if you are not vegan, you can still benefit from using sugar as your primary sweetener for your jar spells as well.

A simple jar spell may include a written petition or photos while a complex one may include a long list of ingredients, including personal matters, a written petition, and pictures that correspond explicitly to your intentions. It's up to you. Trust your intuition and allow the elements meant for you to use and be a part of your honey jar spell.

Here's an easy and quick formula for how to use a honey jar, specifically for attracting new money toward you.

THE MONEY HONEY JAR CANDLE RITUAL

Honey jar

Honey

small container

Photo of yourself

Green pen

Blank check or bank slip

Several drops of Fast-Money Oil (see page 133)

Business card

Sugar bag, bank deposit slip, or parchment paper

Sharpie

A pinch of money-drawing herbs (dried)

Personal matter

A sprinkle of cinnamon powder

A dusting of sugar

Green mini taper candle

Taper candle

2 paper bags or cloths

pinch of sea salt

Human (a candle in the shape of a human figure) or money candle

Directions

1. Begin on a Monday, Wednesday, or Friday. Open the lid of your honey jar, pour the honey into a separate container, and set the honey aside.

2. Write your intentions on your photo (examples: new job opportunity, promotion, success, etc.) in capital letters on the third eye (forehead), eyes, and mouth. Make sure there is no one else in the photo. Place the photo inside the now-empty honey jar.

3. Take your blank check or bank slip and write the amount of money you want to obtain on it. Anoint your check with money oil. Fold it toward you three times, then place it inside the jar. Recite: "With God's blessing, may this amount of money continuously flow to me now and always from all directions and forms."

4. Take your business card and anoint it with money oil. Place it in your jar say, "With God's blessing may this amount of money continuously flow to me now and always from all directions and forms."

5. Make your personal handwritten petition, if desired, by ripping off a square piece from a sugar bag or brown bag or using a bank deposit slip from your bank (this paper is infused with money energy!). If none of these are available, use a parchment paper and proceed with the following:

* Using the green pen, write your full birth name nine times.

* Turn the paper ¼-inch toward you and write your main intention on it, crossing your name nine times.

* Write your command around your name in cursive and your intention in a circle. DO NOT lift your pen until you connect your last letter with the first initial letter. For example: I am a magnet to money, come to me now.

* After you complete the circle of your commands, dot your I's and cross your T's.

* Draw a complete circle around your command and name with a sharpie.

6. Dress the four corners and center of the petition with your oil. Place a pinch of the herbs in the center of your petition and dress it again with a few drops of the oil. Place any personal matter items onto the center of the paper.

7. Now, add some cinnamon and sugar and say, "With God's blessing, may my intentions serve my highest good and may this amount of money continuously flow to me now and always from all directions and forms."

8. Fold the paper-petition toward you three times and place it inside the honey jar. Next, place your remaining herbs in the jar, calling on the energies to help you with your intentions. When you are done, seal the lid on the jar.

9. Prepare your green candle by inscribing it with your full name, date of birth, and command. Anoint it with your oil. Attach the candle to the top of the lid by melting the bottom of the candle and holding it for a few seconds to the lid until it hardens. When you are ready, hold your hands over the candle, focusing on your intention and desires.

Finally, light the candle with the taper candle and pray using Psalm 23 or a prayer of your own.

10. Let the candle burn out on its own and inspect any remains for signs. Repeat the candle-burning process with a new ritual candle each Monday, Wednesday, and Friday for three weeks at 7 p.m., if possible. Once the candle is completely done, give thanks and put it in a paper bag or cloth with a pinch of sea salt. This will protect your intentions afterward. You may throw away or bury it into the earth.

11. Inscribe your human or money candle with your full name, date of birth, and command. Anoint it with money oil. Place the candle on top of your honey jar on the last day, or burn it alone. Burn this candle three times a week (Monday, Wednesday, and Friday) or every Thursday at 7 p.m. Once the candle is completely done, give thanks and put it in a paper bag or cloth with a pinch of sea salt. This will protect your intentions afterward. You may throw away or bury it into the earth. Do what you feel intuitively, believe in your power, and continue to master your craft.

SPIRIT DOLLS

In the rootwork tradition, spirit dolls, also known as "voodoo dolls" or "doll babies," are made out of a variety of materials, including cloth, herbs, roots, and straw. Each spirit doll resembles the individual's appearances and needs, whether that's yourself or someone else. Some dolls are handmade or premade with clay, cloth, and even wax. You can carve and shape a spirit doll into the form of a human's body. Alternatively, image candles shaped as people will suffice as well for any rituals and spells.

You can use this form of magick to attract what you need for any area in your life. There is also an option to use a spirit doll as a surrogate for healing practices such as energy healing, laying of the hands, or reiki, cutting cords, and even reversing curse spells back to the sender. Some people even use spirit dolls for domination purposes over justice matters, love, and money. Please consider that everyone has free will, and interfering with it is up to you. I don't suggest it unless you have their consent, they are working beside you, and you are serving their highest good.

During my childhood years, I was snooping around my dad's work area, opened up a drawer, and found something fascinating. It was a spirit doll. I picked it up and asked myself, "What is this?" I quickly put it back in, never asking my dad what it was.

I quickly became fascinated with making spirit dolls from scratch. My grandma and I collected and made over 50 dolls altogether. As time passed, I got too busy with the typical teen life, then college. My grandma's health began to decline and so did the health of the dolls. The upkeep was too demanding, and my grandma eventually had to give away some. Right before COVID-19 hit in February 2020, my beloved grandma transitioned to the spirit world. The last of my grandma's spirit doll collection was preserved by my uncle Big Dee. I am very grateful because I am looking forward to the day that I will be able to retrieve them and bring them home with me.

Are you interested in spirit dolls? Try making your own from scratch to really embrace your abilities and craft, or visit your local botanica or new age shop for premade dolls.

Here is an easy way to make a spirit doll.

CLOTH SPIRIT DOLLS

Pen

Cloth fabric

Scissors

Sewing kit

Stuffing (cloth, herbs, or straw)

Dried herbs related to your goal for creating this doll

Personal matters (hair, nail clippings, petitions, photos, etc.)

White linen

Directions

1. Pray over all of the ingredients and materials before preparing a spirit doll.

2. Draw an outline of a human body on the fabric used by the individual the spirit doll will represent or on brand-new fabric, then cut out double pieces.

3. Sew the pieces together with the proper color of thread that fits your intention, forming the human body together and leaving a section toward the top of the head open.

4. Stuff your doll with any stuffing material.

5. Add in the herbs and any personal matters.

6. Sew the remaining opening closed.

7. Wrap the doll in clean white linen and place it in area where no one else will touch the doll.

8. Store the doll until you are ready to use it for a ritual or spell.

THE SEVEN CHAKRAS

The Seven Chakras are divine energies that pulse throughout your body. Each chakra represents one color and associates with special aspects of human awareness.

The **Root Chakra** is located at the base of the spine. It represents a vibrant red, encouraging vitality and self-assurance. The color red provides earthly power to your soul, body, and mind. The Root Chakra is powerful when supporting Aries, Taurus, Scorpio, and Capricorn.

The **Sacral Chakra** is located in the lower abdominal region below the navel. It represents the color orange, supporting harmony and self-expression. Orange chakra candles enhance feelings of sensuality and emotional intimacy. The Sacral Chakra is powerful when supporting Cancer, Libra, and Scorpio.

The **Solar Plexus** is located below the navel. Associated with a sunny yellow, this chakra represents will-power and heightened intelligence. This chakra candle is used to encourage confidence and strengthen your physical energy. The Solar Plexus is powerful when supporting Leo, Sagittarius, and Virgo.

The **Heart Chakra** is located in the center of your chest. It represents the color green, the center of one's being, and serves as a hub of emotional and spiritual energies. It covers the heart and circulatory system, the essence of life. Green draws in healing energies and assists the release of heartaches and regret, opening up the soul to new opportunities. The Heart Chakra is powerful when supporting Leo and Libra.

The **Throat Chakra** is located at the center of the throat. The sky blue color of The Throat Chakra corresponds with personal expression, the ability to listen effectively, and the ability to communicate clearly through speech and the written word. Blue has a calming effect that allows us to connect to higher thought processes and express them. The Throat Chakra is powerful when supporting Gemini, Aquarius, and Taurus.

The **Third Eye Chakra** is located between the eyebrows at the center of the forehead. It is associated with the color indigo and connects us to intuition, spirituality, creativity, and greater understanding. Indigo is a deeply spiritual color that unites the earthly red with the spiritual blue. The Third Eye Chakra is powerful when supporting Pisces, Aquarius, and Sagittarius.

The **Crown Chakra** is located above the crown of the head and is associated with the color white or violet. White signifies pure spiritual energy of the highest realms. Violet has been used since ancient times to depict royalty and higher spiritual wisdom. This chakra connects the soul with the universe and increases creative imagination, heightens intuition, and promotes greater understanding. The Crown Chakra is powerful when supporting Capricorn and Pisces.

THE SEVEN CHAKRA CANDLE

This candle holds aspects of human awareness associated with the Seven Chakras and will help you heal and strengthen your chakras. Use the chakra candles to bring greater focus to your energy healing work. Cleanse and balance the chakras often to promote wellness in body, mind, spirit, and soul.

Pen	Salt
Chakra candle	Taper candle
Candleholder or plate	Snuffer or spoon
Parchment paper	Paper bag
Oils of choice	

Directions

1. Inscribe your full name and date of birth, or the receiver's information, writing from the base upward on the candle.

2. Place your candle in a candleholder or stand it up on a plate.

3. On the parchment paper, write your intentions for each chakra, anoint it with oils, and place that underneath the candle or candleholder.

4. Surround your candle with a circle of salt.

5. Light your candle with a taper candle, say your prayer, and recite your intentions.

6. Burn one chakra color a week on a daily basis around the same time for a minimum of five minutes. Use this time for healing and focusing on that specific chakra. Rub your hands together to generate the healing powers of energy and place your hands on the chakra area throughout the ritual.

Do not blow out your flame. Snuff it out with a snuffer or use a spoon when you need to put your ritual to a pause.

7. Once the candle completes, observe the shapes of the wax remains for signs and symbols you may recognize or that speak to you.

8. Give thanks and put the remains of the candle in a paper bag or cloth with a pinch of sea salt. This will protect your intentions afterward. You may throw away or bury it into the earth.

Remember, do NOT blow it out! It will blow away your intentions.

ARCHANGEL MICHAEL CANDLE RITUAL

This candle is for blessings, protection, and spiritual work. You may also use this candle for any prayer and desire you wish for Archangel Michael to assist you with.

Archangel Michael candle

Candleholder or plate

Pen

Parchment paper

Photo of self

Salt

Taper candle

Snuffer or spoon

Paper bag or cloth

Directions

1. Place the Archangel Michael candle in a candleholder or stand it up on top of a plate.

2. Write your intentions for Archangel Michael on the parchment paper and place that underneath the candle or candleholder.

3. Place your picture under the candle or candleholder.

4. Surround your candle with a circle of salt.

5. Measure and mark your candle in equal parts to burn it over a period of time or light it daily for at least 15 minutes until it's complete.

6. Light your candle with a taper candle, then recite the Archangel Michael prayer and your intentions.

Do not blow out your flame. Snuff it out with a snuffer or a spoon when you need to put your ritual to a pause.

7. Once the candle completes, observe the shapes of the wax remains for signs and symbols you may recognize or that speak to you.

8. Give thanks and put the candle remains in a paper bag or cloth with a pinch of sea salt. This will protect your intentions afterward. You may throw away or bury it into the earth on your property.

THE POWERFUL HAND CANDLE RITUAL

Expand your extrasensory perception with a concentrated meditation ritual to activate your sixth sense. Put all mundane thoughts out of your mind and repeat the provided meditation prayer softly until a sign or vision comes into being. This is a joyful ritual, so if you feel called to move, dance, chant, pray, or sing, by all means, please do so! If you are new to magick or find your psychic abilities aren't as sharp as they once were, this is the ritual for you.

Your third eye is the center of your psychic self and rules your divine given abilities to use your intuition, clairvoyance, telepathic abilities, and more.

Perform this ritual during the evening under the moon. Choose a color that best fits your intentions.

The powerful hand color associations:

* Burn a white hand and blue eye for evil eye protection.
* Burn a green hand and black/gold eye for a helping hand ritual for financial help.

✳ Burn a black hand and gold/purple eye for third eye activation and strength.

Pen

Taper candle

Candleholder or plate

Parchment paper

Salt

Snuffer or spoon

Paper bag or cloth

Directions

1. Inscribe your full name and date of birth, or the receiver's information, toward the base of the candle going up.

2. Inscribe your petition (wish, command, or prayer) going upward on the candle or gently on each finger.

3. Place your candle in a candleholder, or have it stand on top of a plate.

4. Write your intentions on the parchment paper and place the paper under the candle.

5. Surround your candle with a circle of salt.

6. Now recite your intentions, a chosen prayer, or the following meditation prayer while lighting your candle, during and at closing.

Recite three times:

By the power of light

The energies through my flames

Assist me to visualize the world in between

Reveal my mind's eye

Release my sixth sense

Open my sight to see the unseen

And ensure that I'll never forget

There's a world beyond me

Bring it forth within view

Show to me that I have not yet seen

And tell me things I never knew.

7. Light the candle for 15 minutes each day until it burns out completely. Do not blow out your flame. Snuff it out with a snuffer or use a spoon when you need to pause your ritual.

8. Once the candle completes, observe the shapes of the wax remains for signs and symbols you may recognize or that speak to you.

9. Give thanks and put the remainder of the candle in a paper bag or cloth with a pinch of sea salt. This will protect your intentions afterward. You may throw it away or bury it into the earth.

Remember, do NOT blow it out! It will blow away your intentions.

THE GODDESS CANDLE

Discover your inner goddess. She creates, stimulates, and rejuvenates from within you, even when you forget to look for her. She will always be there surrounding you in all directions, shapes, and forms. She is air. She is earth. She is water. She is fire. She is passion. She is wisdom. She conquers challenges and is full of joy. She is your mind. She is your body. She is your soul. She is love, and she is light. She is you.

Pen

Candle of choice

Candleholder or plate

Parchment paper

Oils such as the Attract and Desire Oil (page 128) or Holy Oil (page 129)

Salt

Taper candle

Snuffer or spoon

Paper bag or cloth

Directions

1. Inscribe your full name and date of birth, or the receiver's information, along the base of the candle going upward.

2. Place your candle in a candleholder, or have it stand on top of a plate.

3. Write your intentions on the parchment paper, anoint it with oils, and place it underneath the candle or candleholder.

4. Surround your candle with a circle of salt.

5. Light your candle with a taper candle, say your prayer, and recite your intentions.

6. Do not blow out your flame. Snuff it out with a snuffer or spoon when you need to pause your ritual.

7. Once the candle completes, observe the shapes of the wax remains for signs and symbols you may recognize or that speak to you.

8. Give thanks and put the remainder of the candle in a paper bag or cloth with a pinch of sea salt. This will protect your intentions afterward. You may throw it away or bury it into the earth.

Remember, do NOT blow it out! It will blow away your intentions.

THE NEW LOVE CANDLE RITUAL

This candle is used for bringing all forms of new love toward you.

Honey

Jar

Photo of yourself and/ or your lover

Red pen or red sharpie

Sugar bag, brown bag, or parchment paper

Several drops of Attract and Desire Oil (page 128)

Personal matter	Candle holder
Pinch of love-drawing herbs (dried)	Salt
	Taper candle
Pinch of cinnamon powder	Paper bag
Pinch of sugar	

Directions

1. On a Monday, Wednesday, or Friday, pour your honey into a jar and set it aside.

2. On the photo, write your full name with the red pen or red Sharpie in capital letters on the third eye (forehead), eyes, and mouth. Make sure there is no one else in the photo. Place the photo inside jar.

Alternatives:

* For new love: Making sure to use your photo, follow the above directions, replace your name with "New Love Come to Me Now."

* You may also write the qualities and traits you are looking for in a lover on your photo.

3. To make your personal handwritten petition, rip off a square piece from a sugar or brown bag. If these are not available, use a piece of parchment paper.

4. Using the red pen, write your lover's full birth name, if known, nine times, or write your name nine times for new love.

5. Turn the paper ¼-inch toward you and write your full birth name, crossing your lover's name nine times, or write "New Love Come to Me Now" or a command that best fits your intentions.

6. Write your command in cursive around your name, and your intention in a circle. DO NOT lift your pen until you connect your last letter with the first initial letter. For example: New love meant for my highest good, come to me now.

7. After you complete the circle of your commands, then dot your I's and cross your T's.

8. Draw a complete circle around your command and name with a Sharpie.

9. Dress the four corners and center of the petition with your oil. Place a pinch of herbs in the center of your petition and dress them with a few drops of the oil as well. Add any personal matter items onto the herbs. Now, add some cinnamon and sugar and say, "With God's blessing may my intentions serve my highest good, and may this new love flow to me now."

Fold the paper petition toward you three times and set it aside.

10. To prepare your candle, measure it in three equal parts, leaving slight marks on the candle that are visible.

11. Inscribe the love candle with your full name, date of birth, and your command.

12. Anoint it with your oil.

13. Place the petition underneath the candle or candleholder.

14. Add a circle of salt around your candle to protect the energies.

15. When you are ready, hold your hands over the candle, focusing on your intention and desires. Light your candle with a taper candle, say your intentions, and recite a prayer:

"With God's blessing, may my intentions serve my highest good, and may this new love flow to me now."

16. Light the candle for three days at the Venus hour (see page 219) that best serves your schedule.

17. Let the candle burn out on its own and inspect any remains for signs.

18. Repeat the candle-burning process each Monday, Wednesday, and Friday, until the candle is completely done.

19. Once the candle is completely done, give thanks and put it in a paper bag or cloth with a pinch of sea salt. This will protect your intentions afterward. You may throw the remains of the candle away or bury it in the earth.

THE PYRAMID CANDLE RITUAL

Pyramid-shaped candles are used for drawing specific energies toward you.

* For blessing, cleansing, and healing, use a white candle.
* For divination work and spiritual growth, use a purple candle.
* For friendship and romance, use a pink candle.
* For healing and relaxation, use a blue candle.
* For matters of good luck, money, and success, use a green candle.
* For matters of love, use a red candle.

Pen	Salt
Pyramid candle	Taper candle
Candleholder or plate	Snuffer or spoon
Parchment paper	Paper bag or cloth

Directions

1. Inscribe your full name and date of birth, or the receiver's information, going upward on the candle.

2. Place your candle in a candleholder or stand it up on top of a plate.

3. Write your intentions for each chakra on the parchment paper, anoint it with oils, and place it underneath the candle or candleholder.

4. Surround your candle with a circle of salt.

5. Prepare to light your candle for seven minutes the first night and eleven minutes the next night. You will alternate the lighting times until the candle burns out. If you feel called to burn the candle in one sitting or a different burning time, please do so.

6. Light your candle with a taper candle, then say your prayer and intentions.

7. Do not blow out your flame. Snuff it out with a snuffer or spoon when you need to put your ritual to a pause.

8. Once the candle has burned completely, observe the shapes of the wax remains for signs and symbols you may recognize or that speak to you.

9. Give thanks and put the remains of the candle in a paper bag or cloth with a pinch of sea salt. This will protect your intentions afterward. You may throw it away or bury it in the earth.

Remember, do NOT blow it out! This will blow away your intentions.

CHAPTER 16

✳

DIVINATIONS

✳

In the rootwork tradition, divination is a technique used to gain information about the past, present, and/or future. Not all rootworkers use the same divination techniques. Some focus on their intuitive and psychic abilities skills while others use divination tools or other skills to complement and enhance their techniques. The common divinations tools that you'll find easily today are angel cards, bone readings, candle settings, oracle cards, pendulum readings, playing cards, and tarot cards.

CARD DIVINATIONS

When I was a child, a gifted healer and spiritual advisor named Mrs. Lee quickly caught my attention when I realized that she was using regular playing cards just as a tarot reader would use a tarot deck. I remember whispering into Grandma Mary Ree's ear saying, "Grandma we use those for Go Fish!" Mrs. Lee was phenomenal! Fast forward to my mysterious, low-key secretive and rebellious teen years, when my dad would often consult her about my whereabouts and the people I kept close. She nailed it every time, and there was no denying her legitimacy in being a gifted psychic.

The use of playing cards is very common, but not as much oracle or tarot cards. If you never heard of using a simple deck of playing cards, try learning the meaning of the cards first. Start with the colors, suits, numbers, and variety of spreads to use for divination. If you feel called to learn this type of deck or any other card divination technique, remember it takes time to understand fully.

If you are interested in purchasing a deck, find one that attracts you. Once you receive it, pray over it, keep it in a white cloth bag, and infuse it with your energy before actually using it. Set aside ample time in your day to learn something new. I highly recommend using a notebook to write down notes during your card divination journey. Over time, you will develop a relationship from shuffling and meditating with your cards on a daily basis.

CANDLE SETTINGS

The rootworker performing candle settings prepares candles and petitions, and pairs the spell with proper conjured oils, herbs, minerals and other forms of objects to intensify the powers (see Chapter 14: Candle Magick). These additions are used to be in favor of the seeker's desired outcome. Candle settings range in duration and type. It's up to the rootworker to decide on what type of candle spell or ritual is best to do.

Some rootworkers can interpret the candle flame and movement for signs. See page 204 for more on flame magick. It is also possible to interpret the sound of the flame, the color of the smoke that comes from the flame, and even the wax flow for a deeper understanding. These interpretations are observed throughout the entire candle setting or after the candles are completely done burning on their own.

The most popular candle settings are for all types of love matters, including finding new love, reconciliation, and rekindling an old relationship. The other most popular candle settings are for all types of money matters, including attracting fast money, finding a new job, and good luck with gambling and the lottery.

I grew up watching my dad perform candle settings for his clients and for us. I was fascinated by the flame movements and wax flow. Throughout my practice of candle settings, I've learned how to interpret my own way intuitively. My clients come to me mainly for love and money candle settings.

PENDULUM READINGS

A pendulum is a weight that swings freely from a fixed point. Hold the pendulum between your thumb and index finger, with your elbow slightly bent at your side. Use the hand that feels most comfortable for you. Just relax. It is important to let the natural vibration of your own body move through your hand to the pendulum. The pendulum will show you the answer to any yes or no question by picking up and amplifying subtle vibrations from your subconscious, causing the pendulum to swing.

HOW TO INTERPRET YES OR NO

For many people, when the pendulum swings left and right, this can be interrupted as "no." If the pendulum swings to and fro, then this can be interpreted as a "yes." If your pendulum swings clockwise, counter-clockwise, elliptically, or in some other gyration or even stays rigidly still, you must interpret this as best you can.

Start by asking your pendulum something that is true:

"Is my name _____? (Insert your real name)

Note what the response is. This will give you the movement for a "yes."

Now ask your pendulum something that you know is not true:

"Is my name Sage?"

Note what the response is. This will give you the movement for a "no."

Alternatively, to establish how your pendulum works with you, hold the pendulum over a circle and ask the following questions to help you establish how best you will work together.

IMPORTANT TIPS

The pendulum can provide a good second opinion. It uses your own energy, and as such, should not be touched by others who may impart their vibration into the pendulum and thereby reduce reliability. Keep the pendulum with you as much as possible during the first three weeks to have it absorb your energies. Ask the pendulum simple questions that will help build your trust answers. Asking questions that you already know answers to will only result in frustration. The pendulum will learn to resonate with you, within your own energy field. Cleanse your pendulum in saltwater, sage smoke, holy water, or any cleansing protocol you already implement into your spiritual and magickal practice.

Some people get better results holding the pendulum about 1 inch above the open palm of their opposite hand. This opens your energy circuits and creates a biofeedback loop between the energy centers/chakras in your hands. Also, empty your mind of doubts and preconceptions about the outcome of your question. It is important to have a clear mind so the answer is not muddled up by your own thoughts.

Clear the energy from the pendulum after each question by simply lowering the tip for a moment to your hand or other surface. This signals that your question has been answered and you are ready for the next question. Use this technique frequently, especially if your answers seem confusing.

Observe and note the direction of movement following each command.

Show me "YES"	
Show me "NO"	
Show me "MAYBE"	

If movement is weak, say,
"SHOW ME A STRONG _____ (yes, no, maybe)."

Then ask the following test question to understand how you will recognize your answer.

Am I (say your age) _____ years old? You should get your movement for "yes." Then repeat this question, using an incorrect age to check your answer. You should get your movement for "no."

Formulate your own easy test questions to help establish recognition of movement patterns for each answer. Some people who use a pendulum prefer to start the tool in motion before asking a question. I have found that in holding the pendulum still and then asking your question, there is less doubt in the answer to the question.

CONCLUSION

Greetings Beautiful Soul,

This is your time to rise. If you feel that you need to rekindle the light in your soul, it's time to put in work. Don't wait until you have everything. Perfection is not the key. You are the key. Your connection to God is the key.

Your ancestors, angels, and spirit guides are here to steer you along your path toward a higher consciousness. They will lead you to your highest potential as a spiritual being to fulfill your soul's purpose in this human lifetime. Your higher self is calling you. I feel it. I see it and I believe it. Why are you here? God connected us. Now, continue to light the way ahead. Keep your flame burning and nothing can stop you. Nothing can keep you from your goals and desires. Everything that is destined to be yours will come.

Think about it, six months from now, you can be in a completely different mindset and on a different vibration. The frequency of your whole being may shift to another paradigm as you travel through your life's journey. Your finances may elevate and you may start to see all your blessings manifest. Stay dedicated and focused on your goals. Don't forget to stay healthy and fall in love with a spiritual and physical self-care routine that includes the whole of you—mind, body, spirit, and soul.

Keep practicing your craft and create your own book of rituals and spells. I'm looking forward to meeting with you spiritually and virtually. Let's connect and vibe; find me on all social media platforms, especially Facebook/Meta and Instagram @HOODOOGODDESS.

Visit my shop at www.hoodoogoddess.com. Use promo code: ROOTWORK for 15 percent off.

May you be blessed with good health, wealth, love and infinite blessings! Go forth in peace. Ase!

Blessings,

Hoodoo Goddess
Paris Ajana

SUPPLIER RESOURCES

If there are no botanicals, health food stores, or new age stores within your area, visit the following companies online.

The Flowerchild Bruja
www.theflowerchildbruja.com
A flower-powered botanica specializing in sacred smoke wands.

Hoodoo Goddess, LLC
www.hoodoogoddess.com
Magickal and spiritual candles, plus clothing, consultations, wholesale, workshops, and supplies.

Mountain Rose Herbs
www.mountainroseherbs.com
Organic and sustainable products including bulk herbs and essential oils.

NOW Foods
www.nowfoods.com
All-natural beauty and health supplies plus high-quality essential oils.

Studio of Ptah
www.soptah.com
Master craftsman Heru Semahj creates jewelry inspired by symbols of Africa and cultures from around the world.

ACKNOWLEDGMENTS

Every day, I give thanks to my ancestors, especially my beloved Grandma Mary Ree. Thanks to you and Dad for passing down the traditions and trusting me to share them with others. Also, thank you Uncle Dee and Uncle Jamie for sharing our family stories and giving me your support through all my endeavors. I love you all.

Thank you, Dorden, for being there throughout the entire process. Your undivided attention and support have helped tremendously. Also, thank you for trusting me to help guide you along your spiritual journey for the past decade. Your development, gifts, and growth are only going to continue to get stronger. Enjoy your journey, and I love you.

Thank you, Soleil, for inspiring me the most. At age twelve, you completed your first novel. God has truly gifted me a miracle— you my deary are my blessing in this lifetime. Thank you for your encouragement, help, and support; I love you.

Thank you, Mother dear, for believing and praying for me no matter what. Your prayers and altars always receive the highest outcome because of your faith. You continually inspire me spiritually and encourage me to help others.

Thank you, Nova and my beloved Sage, for being my animal guide in this lifetime.

To my friends and family, I appreciate your love and support every single day.

ABOUT THE AUTHOR

Paris Ajana, the founder of Hoodoo Goddess LLC, is a descendant hoodoo candlemaker. She's been a part of the rootwork tradition ever since she was a child. She is also a health-care professional with training as a Reiki master, an oncology reiki practitioner, and a full-spectrum doula. She is a Kemetic practitioner initiated into Shrine of Ma'at based in Harlem, New York, and a MaYoni'at womb yoga teacher specializing in Kemetic womb yoga.

She knows firsthand how to become aligned with the manifestation process by utilizing spiritual and magickal candles and other metaphysical tools; she can work directly with individuals on their spiritual journeys. Advising based on individual needs, the Hoodoo Goddess guides the candle ritual selection, which will assist the individual's growth and, most notably, bring transformation into their daily lives.

Visit www.HoodooGoddess.com for ritual candles, tools, candle magick workshops, consultations, energy healing, and more! Connect on Instagram @HoodooGoddess.